Crafting Leather Totes, Backpacks & Bags

Detailed Patterns & Step-by-Step Instructions for 18 Projects

Author: Yoko Ganaha (PIGPONG)
Supervision: TAMURAKO

An Easy-to-Understand Primer
Patterns Contain Hole Positions for Each Stitch

Introduction

Beef and cowhide can be obtained from the same cow

Consuming meat and conscientiously using cowhide were everyday activities performed by ancient peoples in order to survive.

Cowhide, pigskin, sheepskin, and goatskin—these are valuable by products of animal consumption.

Tannin-tanned leather (vegetable-tanned leather) is produced in much the same way as it was in ancient times, when people used animal **skins for clothing and as shelter for protection from wind and rain.**

About This Book

This book aims to teach practical-sized leather bag making techniques, while omitting processes that only professionals use. It also recommends using special tools for hammering, such as lacing chisels and single-hole punches.

Leather thickness is around 2 mm (1⁄16 in.). In the process of creating long, thin straps, we strive to accommodate differences in leather strength—due to variations in sourcing and leather quality—as much as possible.

Even if we cut leather exactly to a pattern, creating a bag that doesn't warp due to three-dimensional torquing and curved seams would be a very difficult task indeed.

To address this, we included stitching-hole markings on the patterns and we ensured that the leather pieces are aligned by matching up stitching holes. This makes it less likely that seams, especially in the corners, will shift. This, in turn, allows us to create a proper three-dimensional finish.

This is the third installment in a series on vegetable-tanned leather. Even though it introduces leather crafting from the basics up, we have also included larger practical-sized leather items. We hope that even leather workers with a decent amount of experience will find this book useful.

Vegetable-tanned leather is a fascinating material.

When moistened, it can be bent or stretched quite freely.

When dried, it retains its shape.

It's a material that stimulates creativity.

Vegetable-tanned leather is a wonderous material that enables us to make sturdy bags using techniques akin to those found in papercraft.

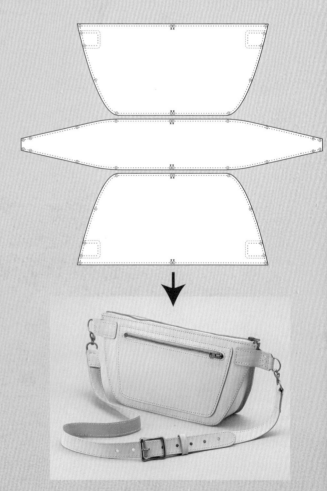

2

Table of Contents

Chapter 1   12
Basic Procedures

Chapter 2   38
Practical Application of Basic Techniques

Shoulder Straps and Handles

Chapter 3

Instructions for Making Various Bags

**No. 11
Circle-Shaped
Handbag
142**

**No. 15
Briefcase
Raised
Pockets
172**

**No. 12
Small
Handbag
152**

**No. 16
Tote/Backpack
Type
182**

**No. 13
Flat Briefcase
158**

**No. 17
Backpack
Satchel Type
192**

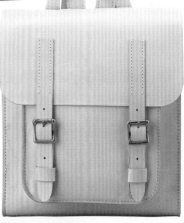

**No. 14
Briefcase Flat
Pocket
164**

**No. 18
Backpack
Briefcase Type
202**

Regarding Tanned Leather

Not unlike meat, animal hides will naturally decompose if left untreated. Removing fat and processing (tanning) hide to prevent decay produces what we call "leather."
Two typical methods of tanning are vegetable (tannin) tanning and chrome tanning.

Tanned Leather

Tannin is a natural substance found in tea.
"Vegetable (tannin) tanning," which has been around for ages, is the term used to describe a tanning method that uses chemicals contained in tree bark.
The primitive nature of this process makes it very time consuming. The various broadly termed "vegetable tanned leathers" are often simply called "tanned leathers."
If worn-out tanned leather is just thrown away, it will just gradually decompose into dirt. This is similar to what happens with dead animals in the wilderness.

Chrome tanning is a tanning method that uses chemicals.
It takes fewer steps than vegetable tanning, and can be industrialized, so most commercially circulated leather products are chrome tanned. Such leather is often dyed or has some surface finishing.
In the narrow sense, only leather that has been tanned naturally, without being processed, may be called "tanned leather."

Natural Vegetable-Tanned Leather

Vegetable-tanned leather is an untreated, natural leather with little oil content. This enhances its ease of use. It's the most popular form of leather in leather crafting, with a pale pinkish cream color. It is also a tough, slightly rigid leather with a good amount of firmness.

Vegetable-tanned leather retains the inherent characteristics of leather, such as being prone to surface scratching, moisture absorption, stretching when wet, and susceptibility to color change due to oxidation.
That being said, it is easy to process, and forming different shapes with this type of leather is a breeze. In addition, when broken-in it becomes soft and much more lustrous. Over years, it gradually changes shades to a nice warm, amber color. Which is to say, natural vegetable tanned leather embodies the authentic feel of broken-in leather.

Since natural vegetable-tanned leather is not treated with any surface finishing, there will sometimes be areas that contain scars. Bug bites, wrinkles, and veins will also be clearly visible. Of course, this all just proves that the leather is an authentic animal skin. If we remain unconcerned with such tiny imperfections, including lightly damaged areas, we can enjoy not only the process of leather crafting itself, but also the everyday use of our very own leather-crafted bags.

Friction and fatigue from daily use—as well as changes caused by exposure to sunlight and the oxidation of natural skin oils / softening oils applied to the leather—will gradually turn the leather a warm amber color.

Brand-new leather

Naturally aged leather

Parts of the Leather

In leather crafting, the front side is called the "grain side," the rear side is called the "flesh side," and the cut side is called the "edge."

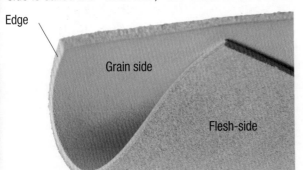

Edge
Grain side
Flesh-side

The grain side of vegetable-tanned leather is easily dented.
Even pressing on the grain side with a fingernail can leave marks.
Since natural vegetable-tanned leather is generally low in oil, supplementing with protection cream is recommended. This will make the leather last longer.

Leather Thickness

You can specify thickness when purchasing your leather. In this book, all items are made of approximately 2 mm (1/16 in.) thick leather.

Leather that has only a flesh side, where the grain side has been peeled off to adjust its thickness, is called "split leather." It is used to increase or reinforce the thickness of a bag or a particular part.
Split leather can be relatively inexpensive and quite interesting, so sometimes it's fun to attempt to create unique works with it.

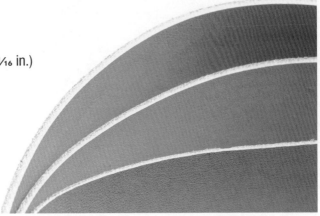

Easily Accessible Leather

Each piece of leather has its own unique set of characteristics. Differences in the tanning process, nature of chemicals used, and type of cattle all contribute to variations in leather. Please be sure to really feel the leather and seek advice from the vendor when selecting pieces to purchase, especially when they will be used for large bags. Also remember that even though the color may appear like this (photo below) at the time of purchase, it will gradually change to a beautiful amber over time.

Here we have a sturdy leather that has been carefully tanned. It has a firm flesh side. Handles and belts can be made with just a single layer of this type of leather, without stitching, as long as it is the correct thickness. This leather is great for making sturdy bags.

This is the most familiar leather in Japanese leather crafting. It has characteristics that are a mix of French and Tochigi tanned leather. It is easy to work with and readily available in Japan.

You will find that this leather is fairly supple (on the flesh side) when compared to others. While durable, it should be noted that even bags made from thick leather can have a gentle finish that fits comfortably in the hand.

Tochigi Tanned Leather

Himeji Tanned Leather

French Tanned Leather

Purchasing Leather

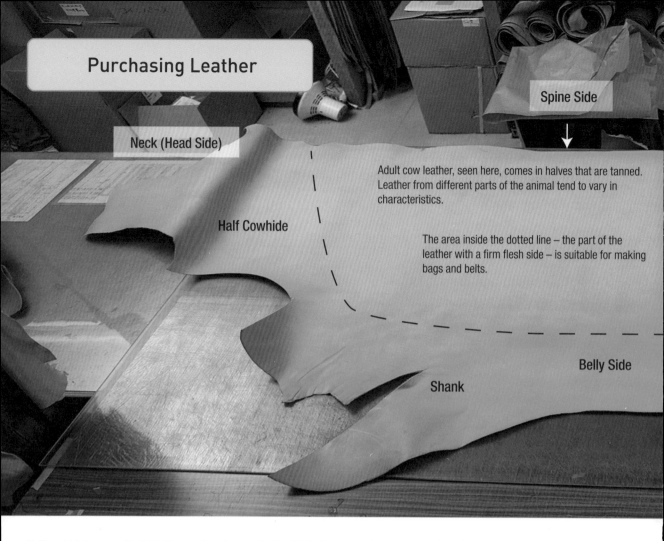

Spine Side

Neck (Head Side)

Half Cowhide

Adult cow leather, seen here, comes in halves that are tanned. Leather from different parts of the animal tend to vary in characteristics.

The area inside the dotted line – the part of the leather with a firm flesh side – is suitable for making bags and belts.

Belly Side

Shank

Half cowhide is more affordable than neatly cut square leather. While it may have irregular parts, brands, or damaged sections from injuries, it offers the joy of creating and the freedom to craft various items.

Cowhide Unsuitable for Bag Making

Cowhide with Uneven Color due to Sun Exposure
Aging will lessen conspicuous differences in color, but avoid extreme differences if possible.

Joints
Areas near joints are stretchy and flexible to allow movement, with fibers running in specific directions. These can distort the shape of the bag, so it's best not to use them for single-piece items.

Coarse Flesh side
Leather can be soft, slightly whitish, and fluffy, especially in the belly region. This area lacks firmness and is prone to wrinkling, making it unsuitable for sturdy bags.

Flesh side

★ These parts are not suitable for items that need to hold their shape, but they are interesting nonetheless. Although bags made from these parts may become distorted, they are still quite durable. You can always create unique items with such parts.

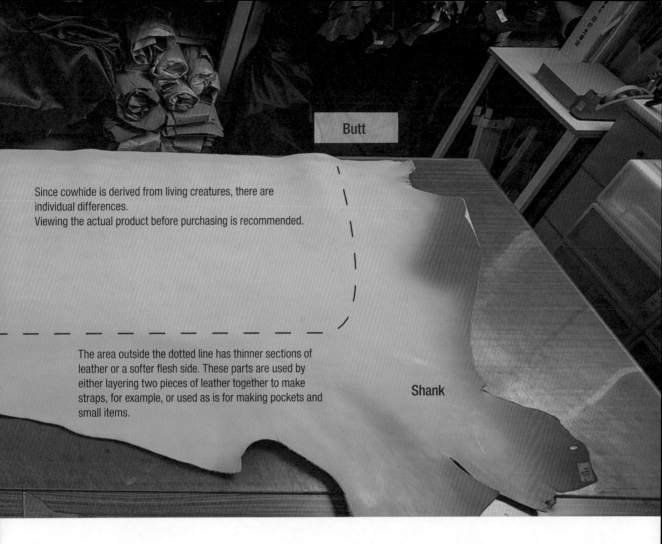

Butt

Since cowhide is derived from living creatures, there are individual differences.
Viewing the actual product before purchasing is recommended.

The area outside the dotted line has thinner sections of leather or a softer flesh side. These parts are used by either layering two pieces of leather together to make straps, for example, or used as is for making pockets and small items.

Shank

Purchasing Off-the-Shelf Leather

Be sure to bring the necessary full-scale patterns and arrange them on the leather in order to make sure it is large enough. How the pattern is placed on the leather and how each item is cut becomes very important. If there are damaged areas, or areas that can be easily stretched, check to see that they are usable or, if possible, to avoid these areas completely.

Since off-the-shelf leather might include difficult-to-use sections, it is recommended to purchase larger pieces while taking into account allowances for cutting and leather distortion.

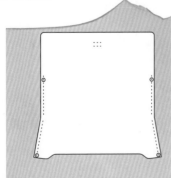

[Leather Measurement Units]

Each hide has a unique shape.

Sometimes "ds" is used as a unit of measurement.

1 ds is 10 cm squared (approx. 4 in. squared).

A ds measures how many 10 cm squared sections (approx. 4 in. squared) will fit in a rectangular-shaped piece of hide.
When pricing is per 1 ds, especially with half cowhide, the usable area—and any damage—affects the calculation. So, it's not always straightforward.

1 ds

10 x 10 cm (approx. 4 x 4 in.)

Tools and Materials

Making Patterns

Glue Stick

Gluing Pattern on Leather

Drafting Tape
Easily removable tape for temporarily securing patterns

Cutting Leather

Vinyl Mat
A thick vinyl mat. Place under leather when cutting

Transferring Patterns

Large Utility Knife
Used for cutting leather

Scratch Awl
Used to transfer patterns onto leather or to align stitching holes to aid in hand stitching

Burnishing the Flesh Side and Edges

Burnishing Agent
Applied when polishing the flesh- side or edges

Glass Burnisher
Used to polish the burnishing-agent coated surface

Single Groove Wood Slicker · Wood Slicker
Used to polish surfaces coated with a burnishing agent

Dresser
A file used to adjust and polish edges

Gluing

*Although adhesives used in this book are clear and transparent, the areas where glue is applied are shown in yellow.

Bond G Clear (Contact Adhesive)
Apply to both bonding surfaces, let dry for a few minutes, then apply pressure to ensure adhesion. Used for bonding pieces of leather to each other and for attaching zippers to leather.

Woodworking Glue
Used to seal stitch ends (p. 35)

Double-Sided Tape, 2 mm Wide
Tape has an adhesive strength that is inferior to glue, but this allows for easy bonding without soiling our leather. (p. 67)

Clips
Convenient for holding glued areas in place. Place a small piece of leather over the glued area and then add the clip. This will prevent scratching.

Punching Stitching Holes

Lacing Chisels

Instructions given in this book are for tanned leather that is approximately 2 mm (¹⁄₁₆ in.) thick and a 5 mm (¼ in.) wide lacing chisel. Stitching holes marked on the patterns are set for 5 mm/ (¼ in.) wide lacing chisel as well. Please be careful; if you use a different size of lacing chisel, the stitching hole intervals won't match the pattern markings.

The four-pronged lacing chisel is used to make straight stitches. The two-prong chisel is used for curved stitches.

The photo shows prong widths that are almost actual size. There are various shapes of shafts.

5 mm / ¼ in.   5 mm / ¼ in.

Single-Hole Punch

Used for punching round holes. Various sizes are available.

Lacing Needle

Used for punching individual stitching holes

Wooden Mallet

Use this for striking the lacing chisel and the hole punch.

Rubber Plate

Place this under leather when punching holes, for example

Stitching

Unwaxed Linen Thread
Manually apply wax before stitching.

Leather Needles
The tip is slightly round.

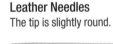

Double-Waxed Thread
Polyester double-waxed thread. Various colors are available.

Wax Block
Wax for arts and craft use

Finishing

Leather Conditioner
A protective cream for tanned leather. Helps keep leather clean and prevents scratches while also softening leather.

Chapter 1

Basic Procedures

This chapter explains the basic process for making a sacoche bag.

Detail

Made from 2 mm (1¹⁄₁₆ in.) thick tanned leather.

Size (Approx.)

24 cm (9½ in.)

B5 (6.9 in. x 9.8 in.)

28 cm (11 in.)

175 cm (68⅞ in.)

Basic Procedures

1 Preparing Patterns, p. 16

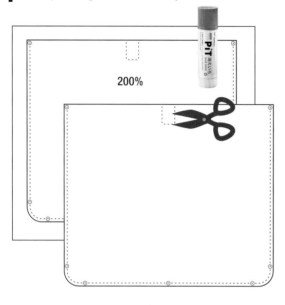

200%

Enlarge patterns in this book to create full-scale patterns.

2 Rough Cutting, p. 20

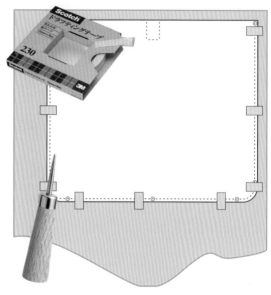

Temporarily paste pattern on the leather and transfer, using a scratch awl.

5 Burnishing the Flesh Side and Edges, p. 26

Apply a burnishing agent to the flesh side and edges, then burnish.

6 Glue Components Together, Then Stic
p. 28

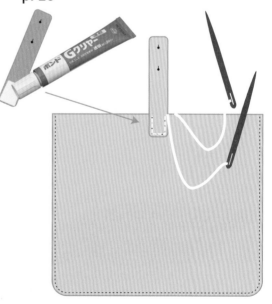

Aligning stitch holes, then glue parts to the main component.
Stitch together.

3 Perforate Stitching Holes, p. 22

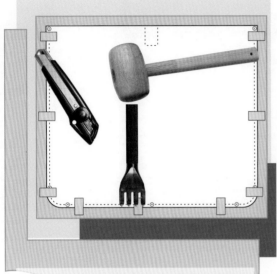

To make hole punching easier, cut the leather slightly wider than the pattern. Then, use a lacing chisel to punch holes in the leather through the pattern.

4 Cutting Leather (Cutting Out the Pattern), p. 24

Cut leather according to the pattern.

7 Glue Main Components Together, Then Sew, p. 29

After attaching parts, glue main components along seam allowance while aligning stitch holes. Then, sew main components together.

8 Finishing, p. 36

Trim stitched-area edges. Moisten leather to stretch and give it a three-dimensional shape. Apply leather conditioner.

Patterns

0 |————————————————————————————————————| 20

Enlarge pattern to 200%.

Patterns provided are 50% reduced.
Use an enlarged copy of the provided patterns.

For multiple items: If no quantity is indicated, the number shown is that needed.

Swivel hook   D-ring   Sam Browne stud

Metal Fittings
Metal fittings are also at reduced scale. Enlarging to 200% shows their actual size.

⑩

Since **shoulder straps** don't fit on the page, some dimensions are omitted.

Adjust **strap length** to fit your body. Refer to chapter 2.

Shoulder Strap — 15 mm / ⅝ in.

← Approx. 1200 mm / 47¼ in. →

Here, we use commercially available leather cut into long, narrow strips for a belt.

Belt loop — Part for holding belt end.

Pattern outline (includes seam allowance)
Cut the leather along this line.

Stitching holes - - - - - -

Encircled stitching hole ⊙
Punch holes with lacing chisel.   This marks a key position when gluing leather pieces!

0 |————————————————————————| 20

D-ring stub position

Belt loop position

D-ring stub position

The thin dashed line indicates a component's position.

●
Sam Browne
stud position

Main component, front

The triangle points to the center of the main component.

16

Patterns

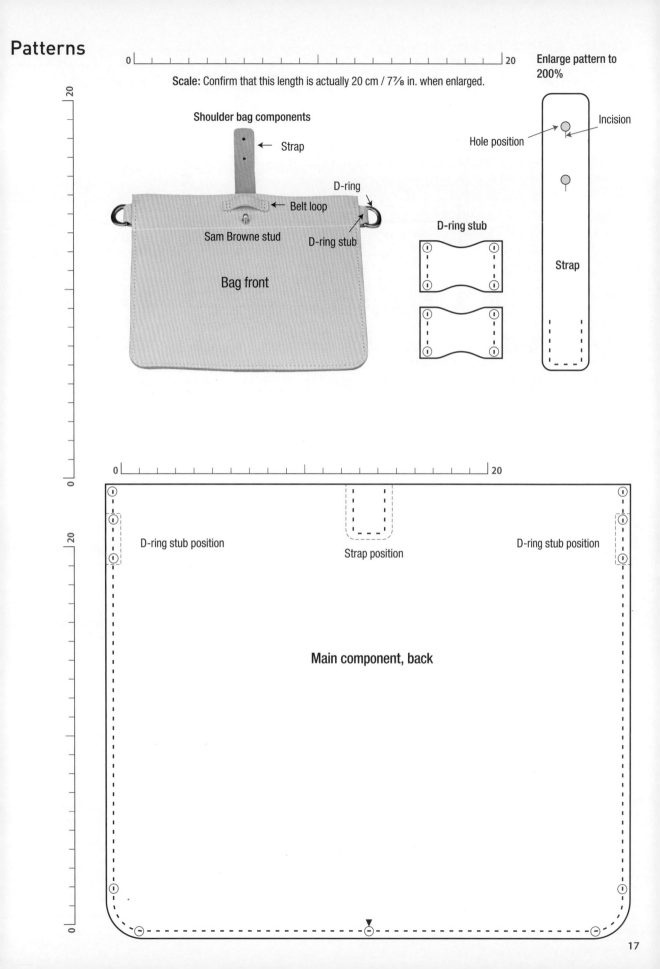

Scale: Confirm that this length is actually 20 cm / 7⅞ in. when enlarged.

Enlarge pattern to 200%

Shoulder bag components

Strap

D-ring

Belt loop

Sam Browne stud

D-ring stub

Bag front

D-ring stub

Hole position

Incision

Strap

D-ring stub position

Strap position

D-ring stub position

Main component, back

Making Actual-Sized Patterns

Patterns are provided at a 50% reduction in order to include as many designs as possible in this book.

Making Enlarged Photocopy of Pattern

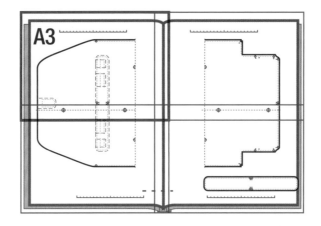

Double-Page Spread

A3 size (11 x 17 in.) copier paper. Make four enlarged photocopies.

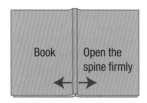

Open spine as much as possible to make photocopies.

If the spine isn't flat, the pattern will be distorted.

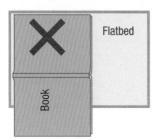

Please be careful! Orienting the book vertically across the copier may result in incorrect photocopies.

Some copy machines may cause distortions along the horizontal and vertical planes.

Given that we align stitch holes during the production process, minor discrepancies can be adjusted. However, if there are serious distortions, you might find it difficult to sew the item correctly.

If you are concerned, please try a copy machine from a store that provides copying services.

When gluing leather pieces together, aligning the center (▲ mark) of the pattern may help remedy the situation.

1 Set left corner of the book in the top left corner of the flatbed and produce photocopy.

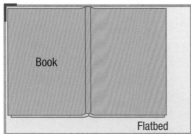

2 Slide book horizontally and align spine with set position. Then produce the photocopy.

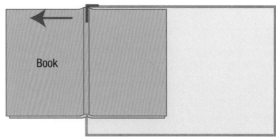

3 Turn book upside down and make photocopy.

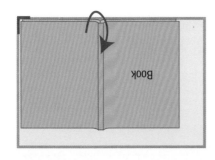

4 Slide the book horizontally and align the spine with the set position, then make a photocopy.

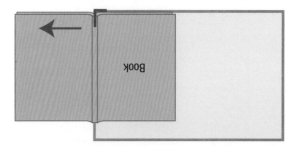

Pasting Patterns on Simili Paper

Simili paper is quite large (788×1,091mm / 31 in. × 43 in., equivalent to duodecimo). It is thicker and sturdier than regular copier paper. It can be purchased at any arts-and-crafts stores.

1 Paste pattern photocopy on simili paper.

2 Cut along outline.

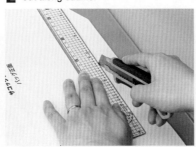

Pattern complete

For Large-Sized Patterns

Large patterns that don't fit on a single page are divided up in order to fit on A3-sized paper. This allows for easier enlargement.

1 Make enlarged photocopies of the pattern.

2 Cut photocopy at marked position.

Marks for aligning pattern segments for gluing
(Note: These marks do NOT indicate center of pattern).

3 On the simili paper, glue the segments of the pattern together while aligning the marks. Then, cut along the outline to make whole pattern.

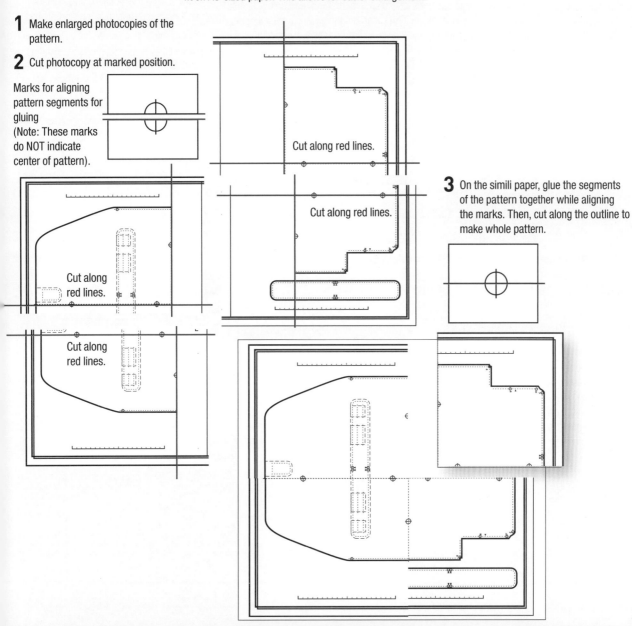

Cut along red lines.

Cut along red lines.

Cut along red lines.

Cut along red lines.

Rough Cutting

Rough-cut large pieces of leather to make them easier to work with.

Prepare Leather

If the leather is warped, moisten both grain side and flesh side with a wet sponge and adjust to flatten. After leather has completely dried, attach patterns.

Arrangement

Attach pattern to grain side of leather with drafting tape (peelable tape used for drafting, for example). Cutting out the necessary number of patterns in advance makes it easier to arrange them on the leather. Doing so also allows us to properly use leather without creating too many remnants.

★ For long parts, such as straps, mark leather directly and then cut along mark. Refer to p. 41.

Small parts should be grouped together and secured, using drafting tape. Punching holes in small pieces of leather can be difficult, so be sure to tape your patterns on a single large piece as shown.

Place pattern for each item on grain side of leather. Then, secure in several places with drafting tape.

Secure drafting tape by folding over the flesh side edge.

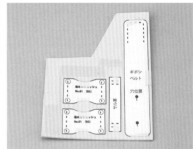

Cutting

Roughly cut leather slightly outside the pattern outline.

Place a vinyl cutting plate under the leather. Always press down on the leather when cutting. Cut with a utility knife. Do NOT press down on the pattern itself, since the paper tends to shift (refer to p. 24 for cutting instructions). After cutting, firmly apply drafting tape around edges on cut side.

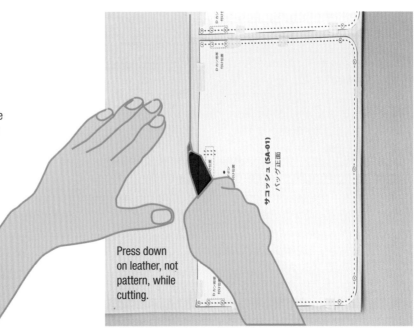

Press down on leather, not pattern, while cutting.

Transferring Patterns

Transfer pattern outline onto grain side of leather with a scratch awl.

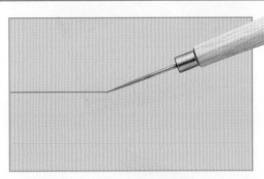

Angle awl tip when scoring lines in order to prevent damage to the grain side. Do not use the awl point!

1

For straight lines, align a ruler with the edge of the pattern and then score.
Do not run over drafting tape, since the scratch awl tip will tear the tape. After punching the stitching holes, and after peeling off the tape, connect the scored lines.

2

For curved lines, lightly hold pattern and score a precise line by following alongside the pattern.

3

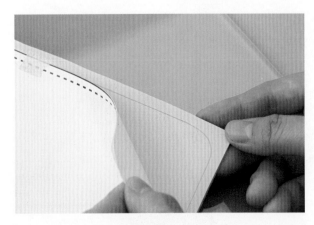

Check for areas where scored lines might be difficult to see.

Punching Stitching Holes

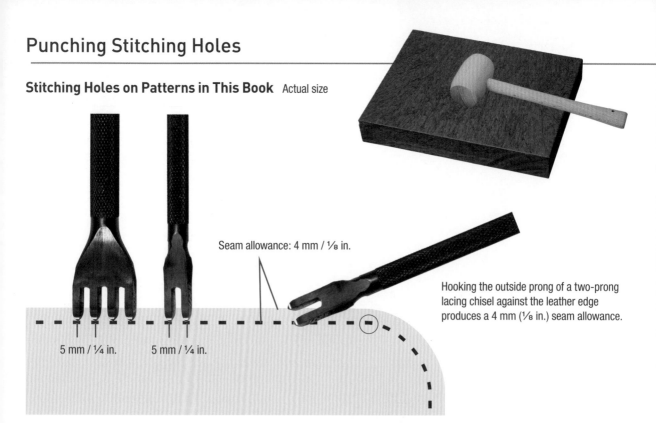

Stitching Holes on Patterns in This Book Actual size

Seam allowance: 4 mm / ⅛ in.

5 mm / ¼ in.   5 mm / ¼ in.

Hooking the outside prong of a two-prong lacing chisel against the leather edge produces a 4 mm (⅛ in.) seam allowance.

Use a 5 mm (¼ in.) wide, four-prong lacing chisel to punch stitching holes marked on pattern. The number of stitching holes is made to match each seam where they join. So, be very careful not to accidentally change the number of stitching holes! A little practice is needed to be able to punch a neat hole straight down through to the back of the leather. For beginners, I would recommend practicing punching holes on a piece of scrap leather.

Hole-Punching Basics

Place leather so that stitches are perpendicular to your body, and then punch holes.

Attempting to punch holes with the leather running parallel to your body may result in a slanted lacing chisel.

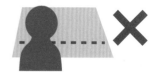

Drafting tape actually has fairly weak adhesive strength, so be sure that the pattern doesn't shift out of position. Tools for punching holes, such as lacing chisels, are very sharp. Work with caution.

Place lacing chisel perpendicular to leather and then strike with a wooden mallet a couple of times to punch holes. Make sure holes are punched all the way through.

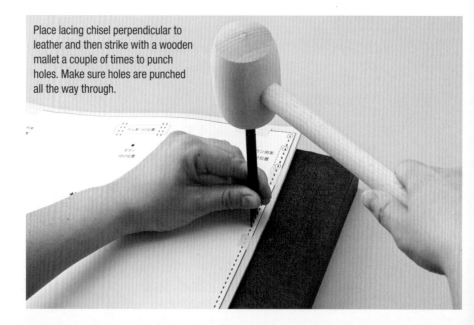

★ If you concentrate too hard on striking the wooden mallet, your lacing chisel hand may move. Firmly hold lacing chisel so that its prongs don't shift. Then strike straight down on the shaft with a wooden mallet.

Straight Stitching Holes

1 Use a four-prong lacing chisel. Place lacing chisel prongs on pattern hole positions. Align outermost prong with the last hole punched and then punch another set of three stitching holes.

2 Place lacing chisel perpendicular to leather.

3 Hold bottom part of lacing chisel and make sure your hand rests on the leather—this will stabilize the chisel and, as a result, the prongs will stay in position.

Last hole punched

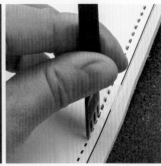

Curved-Line Stitching Holes

Last hole punched

Use a two-prong lacing chisel. Similar to with the four-prong lacing chisel, align outside prong with last hole punched, then punch another set of holes.

Single Stitching Hole

Lacing needle

Arrange lacing needle vertically. Press down firmly and punch individual holes.

Marking

After punching all the holes, pierce circled stitch holes with a scratch awl. Then, turn the leather over and mark the pierced position with a pencil on the flesh side.

Pattern

Mark to use when stitching leather pieces together

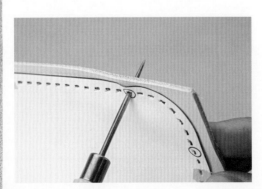

Cutting Out Pattern on Leather

Place vinyl cutting board on a working surface and put leather on top. Then cut with a large utility knife.

Leather is easier to cut compared to paper of similar thickness, but it tends to stretch or distort. That being said, proceed calmly and slowly along lines traced with the scratch awl.

Peel Off Patterns

In the area where draft tape was applied, trace pattern lines with a scratch awl as you peel off the drafting tape.

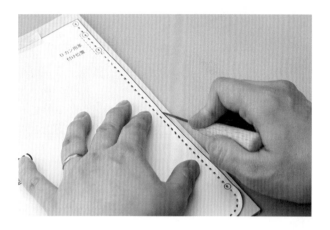

If the lines are difficult to see, just trace again.

Cutting Straight Lines

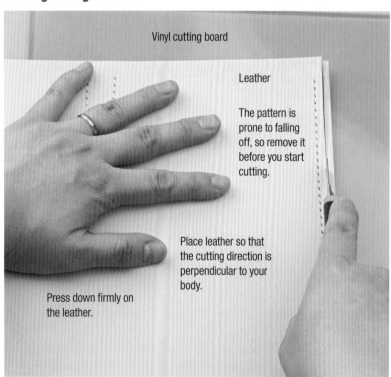

Vinyl cutting board

Leather

The pattern is prone to falling off, so remove it before you start cutting.

Place leather so that the cutting direction is perpendicular to your body.

Press down firmly on the leather.

Carefully and slowly cut along line with a large utility knife.

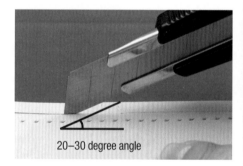

20–30 degree angle

★ Cut leather by holding utility knife so that the blade is angled at 20–30 degrees.
★ If blade angles to the left or right, the edge cut will be slanted. Please pay particular attention when cutting thick leather.
★ Be sure to snap blade off so you are always cutting with a fresh razor.

Cutting Curves

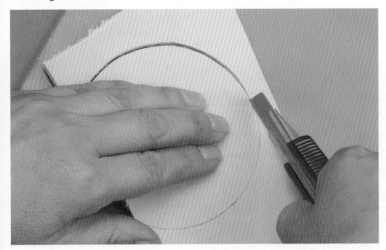

Always keep cutting direction perpendicular to your body by rotating the leather and cutting little by little.

Cutting Corners

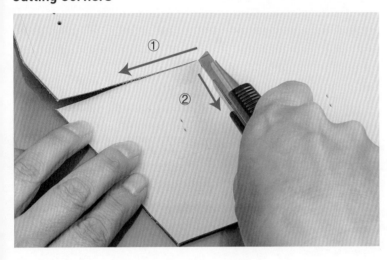

① Firmly place blade at corner and proceed to cut toward exterior.
② Once again place blade at corner and cut steadily along the remaining line.

Caution

Do not use a ruler as a guideline, since the leather is fairly slippery!

Please be sure not to place your fingers in the path of the utility knife!

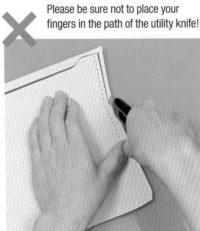

If you cut leather horizontally, the cut line often won't be straight.

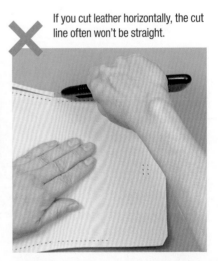

Burnishing Flesh side

Fibers become grainy on the flesh side and come off as the leather breaks in. In order to prevent this, burnish the flesh side by applying a burnishing agent. Do not burnish gluing areas, since burnished surfaces hinder the adhesive action of glue.

1

Take some burnishing agent on a finger and spread it lightly on the leather's flesh side. If burnishing agent is spread out to the edge, it may cross over to the grain side of the leather, resulting in soiling. Apply burnishing agent near the edge with caution.

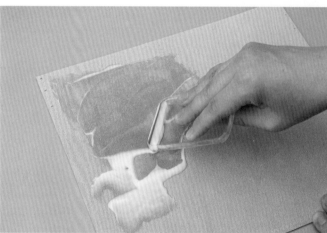

2

Use side of glass burnisher to spread burnishing agent to the edge.

★ Do not apply burnishing agent along seam allowances as they are glued together (applying burnishing agent to the stitching holes will not fill them up). Repeat steps 1 and 2 to spread burnishing agent over entire piece.

Before burnishing

3

Once it reaches a semidry state (not sticky to the touch), polish by sliding side of glass burnisher over the leather. This will help settle the grain side and bring out its shine.

After burnishing

Do not apply burnishing agent on seam allowance.

Burnishing Edges

Smooth out edges.

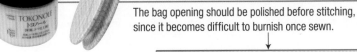

Burnishing Areas

Polish areas marked in red.

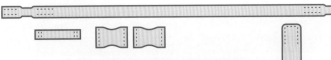

Burnish handles, straps, and parts before attaching them to the main component.

The bag opening should be polished before stitching, since it becomes difficult to burnish once sewn.

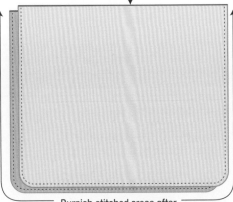

Burnish stitched areas after stitching them together.

1

Take a small amount of burnishing agent on a cotton swab or scratch awl tip and then spread it along the edge. Be careful not to touch the grain side.

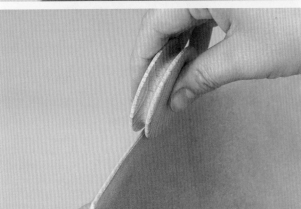

2

After the leather has pretty much dried, begin to burnish the edge.

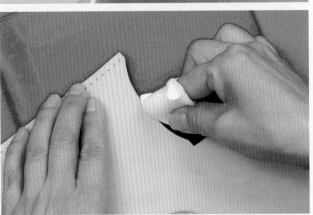

To burnish leather that is approximately 1.5 mm (¹⁄₁₆ in.) thick, just place it on a table and then place a piece of cloth over its edge. Rub both sides after burnishing agent has been applied.

Before burnishing

After burnishing

Gluing

Steps

Glue parts onto main component, then sew.

Glue main components together.

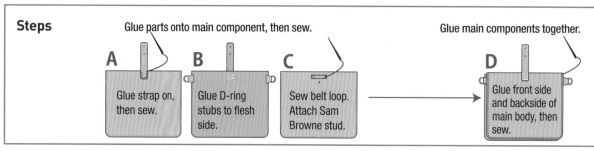

A Glue strap on, then sew.

B Glue D-ring stubs to flesh side.

C Sew belt loop. Attach Sam Browne stud.

D Glue front side and backside of main body, then sew.

Attaching Strap: Step A

1 Apply glue. Carefully apply glue so it doesn't spread to grain side. Let glue dry.

2 Insert needles to align stitching holes.

3 Press firmly to ensure adhesion, and sew.

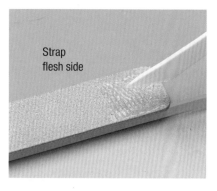

Strap flesh side

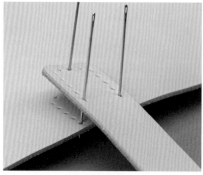

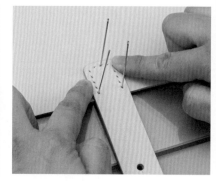

Attaching D-ring Stubs: Step B

1 Moisten leather and fold in half. Apply glue to seam allowance. Let dry. Align stitching holes and glue.

2 Apply glue to seam allowance of both parts and main body. Then, let dry. Insert a needle to align stitching holes between main body and parts. Then glue together.

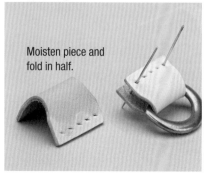

Moisten piece and fold in half.

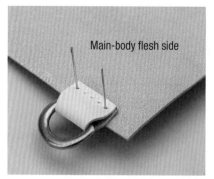

Main-body flesh side

★ Moisten leather with a sponge when folding. This makes it easier to bend.

★ Since D-ring stub will be sewn together along with the main body, it's just glued on at this stage.
Sew after front and back of main body have adhered together.

Attaching Sam Browne Stud: Step C

1 Put shaft of stud base through hole from back side.

2 Apply glue to scratch awl tip, then gently place glue on stud.

3 Place stud over base and tighten the screw.

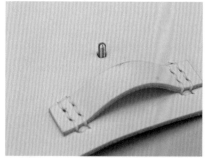

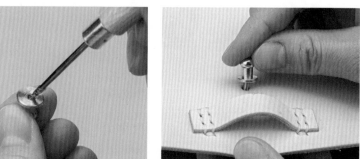

Confirm Stitching Holes

Prior to gluing, make sure the number of stitching holes matches.

Glue

We will use Bond G Clear (Contact Adhesive). Apply it to both sides of the area you want to bond. Let dry for a few minutes and then apply pressure to ensure adhesion.

Gluing Main Body: Step D

1 Apply glue to seam allowance on both front and back of main body, flesh side. Spread towards the edge with a spatula.

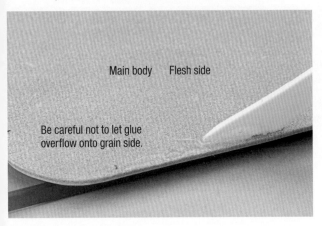

Main body Flesh side

Be careful not to let glue overflow onto grain side.

2 Stack front and back pieces of leather and place a piece of paper between them. Insert needle into marked stitch hole on one side, then force needle into hole marked on opposite side to align holes.

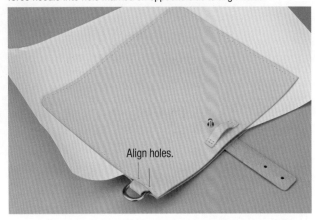

Align holes.

3 For curved areas, align marked stitch holes with needles held vertically. Gently press down on the leather to ensure proper adhesion without displacement.

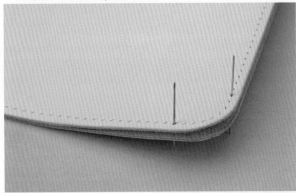

★ Bond G Clear requires application on both target pieces. Apply and then let dry for a few minutes. Remember that the glue won't adhere to paper sandwiched between the pieces, so be sure to move it as you go.
Align stitch holes with a needle while shifting the paper, then proceed with adhesion.

★ After bonding, use an awl to pierce stitch holes and adjust hole positions for easier stitching.

This method is particularly useful for bonding three-dimensional or curved surfaces.

Use ▲ mark in the center of the pattern to help prevent misalignment.

Align hole positions with needles

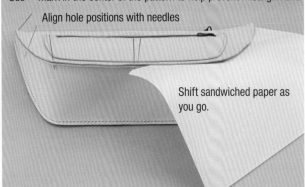

Shift sandwiched paper as you go.

Preparing Thread

Waxing Thread

Leather stitching requires waxed thread. This type of thread resists thinning, even with the large amounts of friction produced during leather crafting.

Thread must be waxed.

Place one end of thread on the wax, cover with a cloth, and then pull the end. Pass the thread over the wax while pressing down on the cloth (repeat 3–4 times).

Waxed thread

This type of thread tends to collect impurities due to it being excessively waxed. Remove excess impurities and wax prior to stitching. Just place the thread on a piece of cloth, pinch it, and pull.

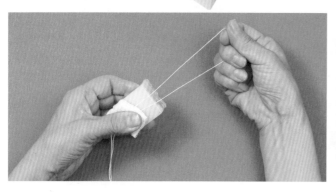

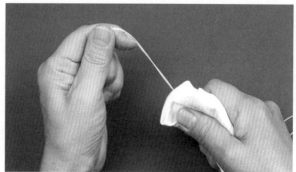

Threading Needle

Leather stitching requires one to continuously pull on the thread, so you must use a special threading method to keep the thread tight.

1 Thread through needle.

Pull about twice the needle length worth of thread through.

2 Hold thread. Loosen thread by twisting. Then, pierce the needle back through the gaps in the thread a few times.

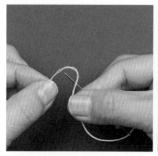

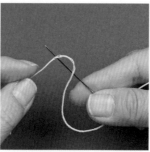

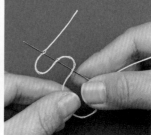

3 Push needle point all the way through the thread.

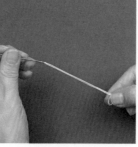

4 Hold longer thread and pull.

5 Adjust.

Starting and Ending Stitching Positions

Decide ahead of time where you want to start stitching. Make sure that your stitch ends at a relatively unnoticeable position so that you can easily dispose of its ends. Examples include the inside of the main body, areas where it's easy to apply glue, or the back of the handle.

Small Parts

Small parts are sewn with a single needle.

End stitching

Begin stitching

Begin stitching at center. Return to center and pull thread to inside.

Bags with Side Seams Sewn Together

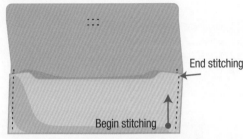

End stitching

Begin stitching

Start stitching from bottom side to ensure that the stitch end is near the opening. This makes it easier to dispose of the thread.

Stitching around Bag Perimeter

For larger bags, sewing from bottom center to the left and right sides, respectively, helps achieve balanced stitching.
Stitching ends near the opening so it's easier to dispose of the thread.

End stitching

Begin stitching

Handles and Shoulder Straps

For long and narrow pieces, where it seems like the thread might run out halfway, begin stitching from center.

Begin stitching

Center

Once you reach this point, finish stitching without cutting the thread.

Attach to bag's main body.

Choose areas that won't get damaged when clamping firmly.

Place on seat of a chair.

Not required, but convenient to have:

Stitching Pony

A stitching pony is a tool used during stitching. It securely holds leather in place, allowing free use of both hands and making it easier to stitch with two needles while pulling tightly on the thread.

Clamping the area near your next set of stitches makes things easier. As you sew, shift the leather position.

Sewing Leather

Thread Length

A rough estimate for necessary thread length is four times the distance to be sewn.

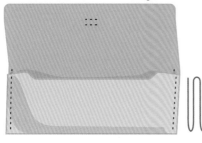

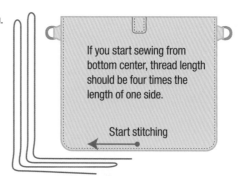

For shorter distances, it's better to have a slightly longer thread.

If you start sewing from bottom center, thread length should be four times the length of one side.

Start stitching

Attach a needle to both ends.

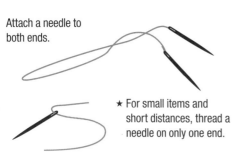

★ For small items and short distances, thread a needle on only one end.

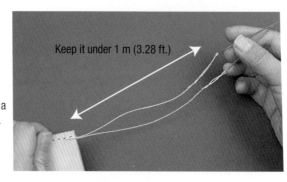

Keep it under 1 m (3.28 ft.)

★ Thread that is too long is difficult to use. So, keep the length of each working thread to just under 1 m (3.28 ft.). only one end.

Begin to Stitch at Corner

1 Initially pass needle through stitching hole just a few holes from end.

2 Double-stitch first stitching hole.

3 Return to where you started.

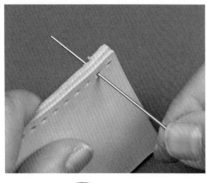

Leather cross-section

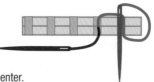

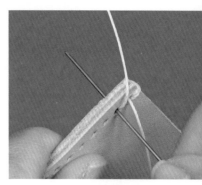

* For clarity, the thread is divided into two colors at its center.

If you begin sewing at the center, double-stitch the initial stitching hole. Then proceed with the remaining holes.

Bag openings and pockets bear the greatest load, so be sure to double-stitch the outermost hole.

Double-stitch the last stitching hole as well, even if it ends on an edge.

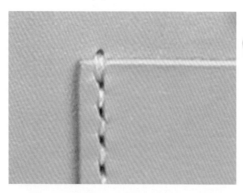

Saddle Stitch

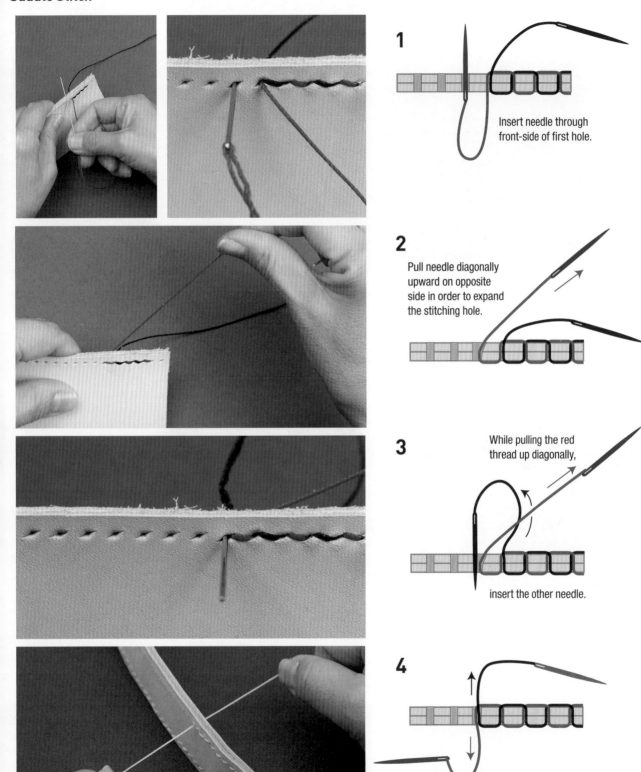

1

Insert needle through front-side of first hole.

2

Pull needle diagonally upward on opposite side in order to expand the stitching hole.

3

While pulling the red thread up diagonally,

insert the other needle.

4

Tighten both threads at same time.

Splicing Thread

1 When you run out of thread, backstitch once from front side and pull thread through to backside. Then cut, but leave enough length to tie.

2 Thread a needle with some new thread and push it through the same hole where you made your last stitch. Continue to sew.

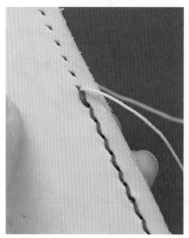

Backstitching for Reinforcement

Areas where parts are attached should be stitched twice for added durability.

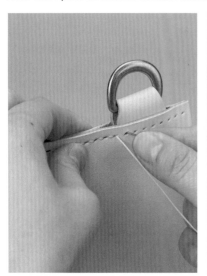

Back one hole and stitch twice.

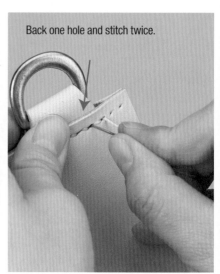
Back one hole and stitch twice.

Stitches on flesh side

Disposing of Thread Ends

1 Start at opening and backstitch (stitch twice). Then, stitch back a few stitches.

2 Finish with thread on inside.

3 Cut thread close to edge.

4 Apply wood glue to stitching holes a few stitches before and after the thread end.

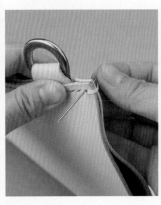
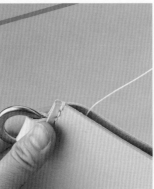

Press firmly down on thread with a leather scrap or wooden handle of your scratch awl.

Flat Area

1 If thread will be too visible, cut after reverse stitching through the other side.

2 Apply glue to several stitching holes, both before and after the trimmed threads.

3 Press firmly with a leather scrap or the wooden handle of your scratch awl to ensure the holes are sealed.

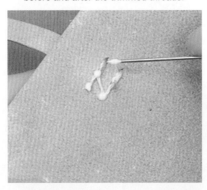

Stitches on grain side

Finishing

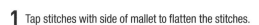

Adjust and Burnish Edges

1 Tap stitches with side of mallet to flatten the stitches.

2 Gradually round off edges with a dresser. Apply burnishing agent to thick areas. Repeat the process of rounding off a few times.

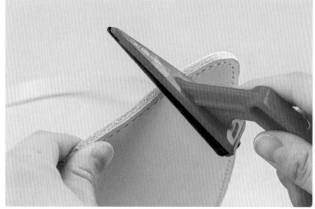

3 Apply burnishing agent to leather edge where two pieces are sewn together. Use a scratch awl or similar tool. Then, lightly polish edges with cloth and let dry.

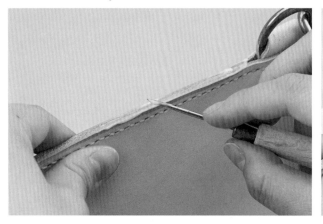

4 Polish edges with a slicker or cloth to produce a shine.
  ★ There are also polishes available that will give the edge a glossy finish.

Shaping

1 Moisten leather with a cloth, or similar material, soaked in water and wrung out.

2 Work from inside, using your hands or a mallet handle to produce a rounded shape. Insert something thick if needed.

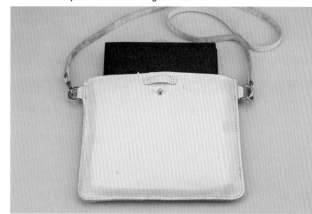

Applying Leather Conditioner

1 Use a soft brush or cloth to remove any dust.

2 Apply a small amount of leather conditioner, using a soft cloth.
Spread it evenly. Once conditioner has dried, polish with a soft cloth.

Wrap cloth around your finger to make it easier to apply conditioner and prevent applying too much at once.

Put on some conditioner.

Remove excess.

Chapter 2

Practical Application of Basic Techniques

In this chapter, we will introduce detailed tips for making parts and constructing the main body. Before beginning production of chapter 3 projects, be sure to read through this section.

Shoulder Straps and Handles

Trace patterns directly on target leather and cut when making long, narrow straps or belts. We have provided basic sizes, but please decide on what works best for you, since sizes differ by individual. Also note that your leather may stretch over time, depending on its firmness at purchase.

We have included two methods to prevent stretching.

Metal Fittings and Zippers

We use only a few types of hardware and one type of zipper. Attachment methods are explained in this chapter.

Regarding Small Leather Parts

Even though we use the general term "tanned leather," in reality there are significant differences in leather characteristics due to subtle variations in the tanning process, differences in parts, and individuality of each hide. That being said, slight adjustments in size may be necessary, especially for the smaller parts in this chapter. After cutting out each piece of leather, it is best to actually position it on the target leather to confirm its size, since these parts have a significant impact on usability.

Modification and Additional Features

This book focuses primarily on efficiently creating bags, while using as few parts as possible. As a result, there are relatively few parts—such as pockets.

This chapter provides methods for adding pockets to the exterior when desired.

It also includes instructions for resizing patterns and extending the size/length of features—such as shoulder straps—in finished products.

Sewing Curved Patterns, Stitching Two-Ply Leather, Adjusting Stitching Holes

Advanced stitching techniques.

Please refer to these techniques when making bags found in chapter 3.

Shoulder Straps and Handles: Length and Style

There are no fixed lengths or specifications for the shoulder strap patterns in this book. That being said, you can adjust handles to any size that is convenient for you. We recommend checking against a bag you already own.

Determining Length

Basic shoulder strap structure

Swivel hook position

Upper shoulder strap (adjust length here)

Approximate strap length when bag is in use

Buckle position

Lower shoulder strap

Swivel hook position

Length when using backpack shoulder straps:

80–95 cm
(31½—37⅜ in.) is common.

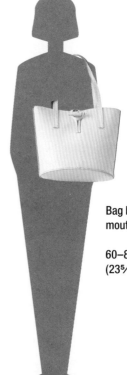

Length when using shoulder strap:

For crossbody use, 120–150 cm (47¼–59 in.) is common.

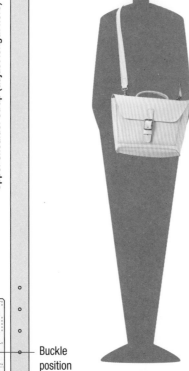

Bag handle length, from bag mouth, when on the shoulder:

60–80 cm
(23⅝–31½ in.) is common.

Choosing Your Own Style

For long, narrow straps, degrees of stretch and deformation will vary on the basis of leather thickness, livestock origin, and location on hide. Choose the piece of leather that best fits your strap.

A Single-layer construction

No stitching

If the leather is strong enough, there's no need to add stitching.

B Single-layer construction

Stitching along edges

If the leather is somewhat weak and prone to stretching, add stitching along edge to strengthen.

C Two-ply construction

Stitching along edges

Two-ply construction is best for creating durable belts. If you prefer thinner straps, feel free to use thin leather for the second layer.
(1 mm [1/16 in.] thick leather is used throughout most of this book.)

Cutting Long, Narrow Straps (for Handles and Shoulder Straps)

Long, narrow straps tend to warp, even when cut using patterns. Instead of roughly cutting, draw lines directly on grain side with a scratch awl. Then cut.

1 Draw lines on belt from one end to the other (including metal-fitting stub zones) on grain side with a scratch awl. Having a grid ruler is convenient for drawing a dead straight line.

2 Cut along the line.

Creating a Simple Handle (Flat Handle)

A For Single-Layer Construction

1 Cut leather to size of handle.

2 Attach pattern with drafting tape.

3 Use a lacing chisel to punch stitching holes.

4 Apply burnishing agent to edges and polish. Place pattern on flesh side and mark positions.

B For Adding Stitching along Edges

1 Place lacing chisel on leather edge and mark a line for seam allowance.
(Lines that are approximately 4 mm [⅛ in.] wide can be marked.)

Portion attached to main body

Portion attached to main body

2 Punch stitching holes along marked lines.

Insert outermost prong into the last hole punched. Then, proceed to punch the subsequent set of holes.

At the end, lightly mark holes with a lacing chisel to adjust spacing between stitches.

3 Apply burnishing agent to edge and polish.
Confirm marks on portions that attach to main body, then add decorative stitches to center portion (i.e., excluding main body attachment points).

Area to be sewn onto main body.　　　　　　　　　　　　　　　　　　　Area to be sewn onto main body.

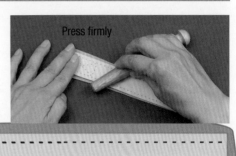
Press firmly

C For Two-ply Construction

1 Glue leather with stitching holes onto a slightly larger piece.

2 Punch stitching holes through to second piece of leather.

Make sure to firmly pierce the backside leather through the holes on the front.

3 Cut away any unnecessary leather.

4 Apply burnishing agent to edge and polish.
Confirm marks on portions that attach to main body, and then add decorative stitches to center portion (i.e., excluding main body attachment points).

Areas sewn onto main body.　　　　　　　　　　　　　　　　　　　Areas sewn onto main body.

Glue handle onto main body, while aligning stitching holes, and then sew on handle.

Making a Folded Handle

1 Punch stitching holes. Then, cut leather according to pattern.

Area where leather is folded in half.

2 Moisten leather where it will be folded, then fold.

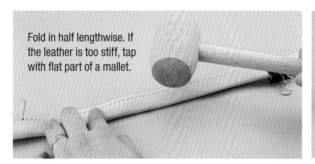

Fold in half lengthwise. If the leather is too stiff, tap with flat part of a mallet.

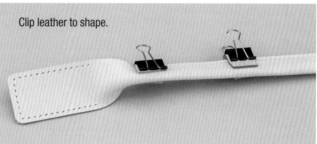

Clip leather to shape.

3 Align stitching holes and glue edges.

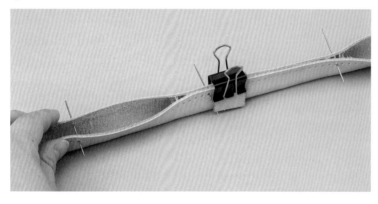

4 Finish stitching center of handle. Apply burnishing agent to edges and polish.

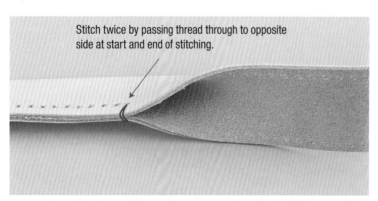

Stitch twice by passing thread through to opposite side at start and end of stitching.

5 While aligning the stitching holes, glue handle on the main body, and then sew the handle on.

Patterns: Shoulder Strap • Bicycle Belt

Common Patterns

- Backpack: Tote Bag Style, Backpack: Briefcase Style, Backpack: Satchel Style (bottom side only)—two shoulder straps for each item

- Camera Bag, Navicular Sling Bag, Square Sling Bag, Messenger Bag—one shoulder strap for each item

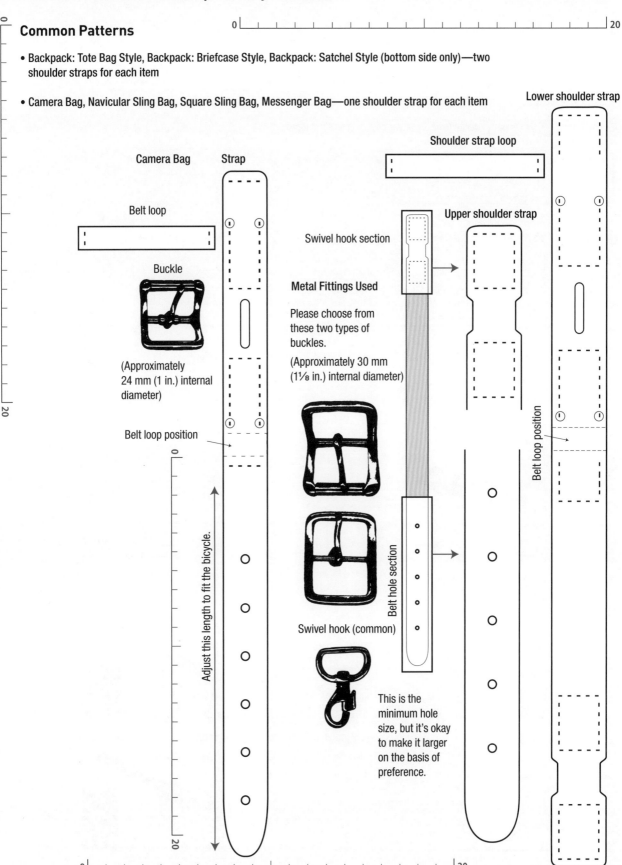

Lower shoulder strap

Shoulder strap loop

Camera Bag   Strap

Belt loop

Buckle

Swivel hook section

Upper shoulder strap

Metal Fittings Used

Please choose from these two types of buckles.

(Approximately 30 mm (1⅛ in.) internal diameter)

(Approximately 24 mm (1 in.) internal diameter)

Belt loop position

Belt hole section

Adjust this length to fit the bicycle.

Belt loop position

Swivel hook (common)

This is the minimum hole size, but it's okay to make it larger on the basis of preference.

Upper Section of Shoulder Strap

1 Mark strap grain side, according to size that includes parts portion, and then cut.

Swivel hook section   Belt hole section

2 Add pattern for swivel hook section to necessary area, using drafting tape.

3 Mark lines along pattern with a scratch awl.

4 Punch stitching holes.

5 Also, add belt hole section, using drafting tape. Mark lines with scratch awl and punch belt holes.

6 Cut along lines.

B   Adding Stitches along the Edges

Upper shoulder strap

Mark line, using two-prong lacing chisel.

Punch stitching holes along lines. Connect ends of stitching holes.

Apply burnishing agent to edges and polish.

For lower part of shoulder strap, cut leather and then punch stitching holes in the same way.
Apply burnishing agent to edges and polish.

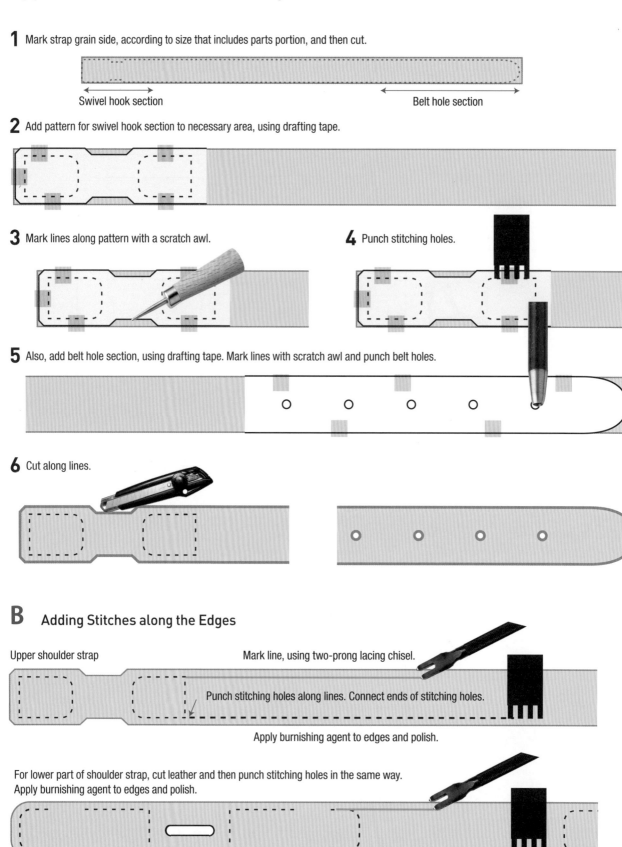

Making Lower Part of Shoulder Strap and Attaching Buckle

1 Punch stitching holes according to pattern and cut.

2 Punch holes with a single-hole punch to make space for buckle pin.

3 Cut leather that connects punched holes.

4 Form belt loop to check size. It's best to have some extra space to accommodate double belt thickness. Sew ends together to form a loop.

5 Thread belt loop through belt.

6 Put buckle through belt and fold leather over buckle.

7 Align stitching holes and sew together.

Stitching complete

Front

Back

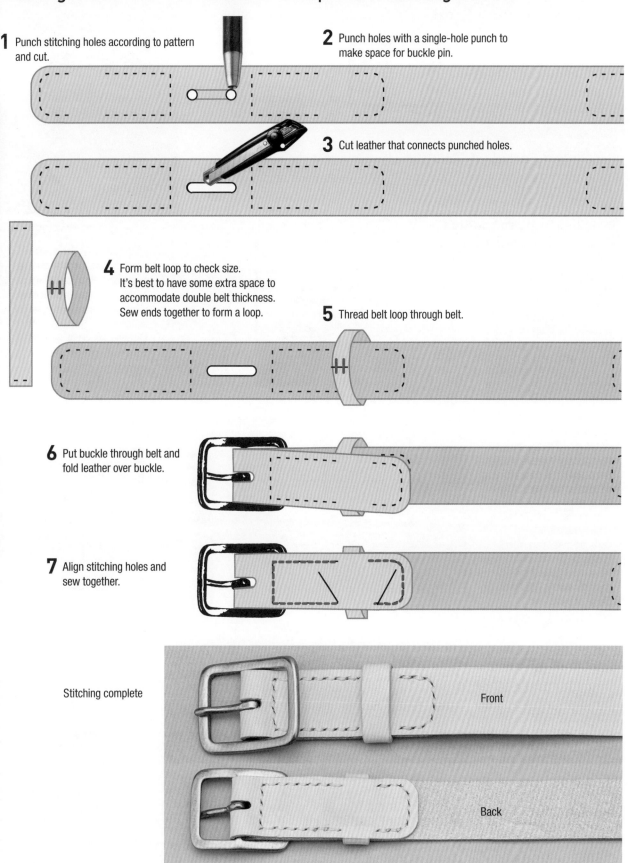

Punching Holes, Attaching Magnetic Clasp and Sam Browne Stud

For the belt hole, use a single-hole punch with a diameter equal to or larger than the pin diameter of the buckle you're using.

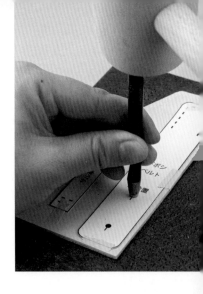

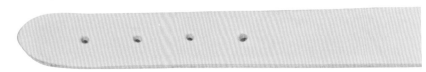

Installing Sam Browne Stud

Screw-on type

This is a metal fitting with a bulbous head. Fasten using a hole punched in your leather strap.

- ★ Best practice for determining Sam Browne stud position is to do so after the bag is complete. Place belt where desired and confirm hole positions before actually punching holes.
- ★ Covering metal parts (back side of stud base) with a thin leather piece provides protection for the contents inside. This ensures peace of mind.

Fastening on Hole Side

Base Side

Make a hole with a single-hole punch and push base through.

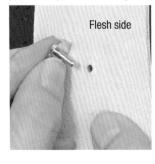

Flesh side

From the other side, place stud over base and tighten screw.

Grain side

On the flap side, use a hole punch to create an opening that is approximately the same size as the stud. Make a slit with a utility knife to facilitate inserting the stud.
Making a small hole with a single-hole punch makes it easier to push the stud head through.

Tighten firmly with a flat-headed screwdriver.

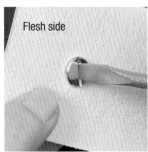

Flesh side

Installing Magnet Clasp

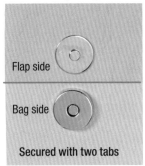

Flap side

Bag side

Secured with two tabs

This is a magnetic metal fitting.
- ★ Covering metal parts on backside with a thin piece of leather protects contents, thus ensuring peace of mind.

Press tabs down on grain side to mark their positions.

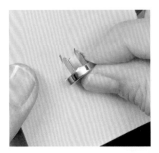

Make slits for tabs to pass through. Push tabs through, add washer, and tightly sandwich leather.

Use pliers to bend tabs. This will secure washer to leather.

- ★ Attach one side first. Then, attach remaining side after confirming hole position by aligning flap with the bag body once bag is complete.

Installing Bag Feet

Attaching bag feet and studs

Feet are used to the lift bag off the floor to prevent soiling. Typically, four feet are attached.

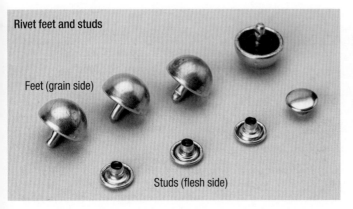

Rivet feet and studs

Feet (grain side)

Studs (flesh side)

Setter
Choose on the basis of stud size.

Punch holes according to foot post size.

Insert bag feet into grain side.

Add stud on flesh side.

Avoid scratching bag feet by placing leather on a towel before striking with a mallet.

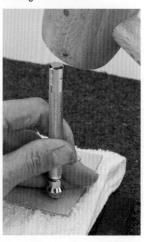

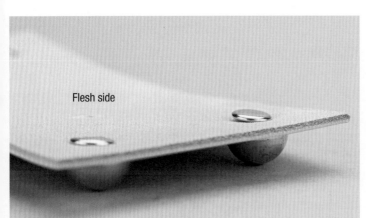

Flesh side

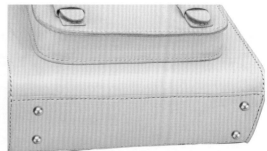

Installing a Zipper

All zippers used in this book are the same size. Patterns in this book have a slot for a zipper that is 12–13 mm (½ in.) wide.

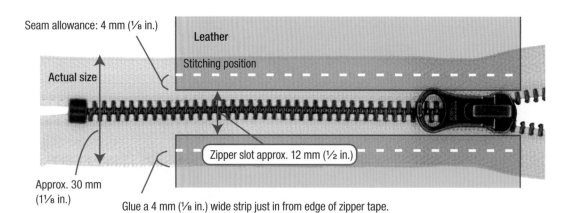

Seam allowance: 4 mm (⅛ in.)

Leather

Stitching position

Actual size

Zipper slot approx. 12 mm (½ in.)

Approx. 30 mm
(1⅛ in.)

Glue a 4 mm (⅛ in.) wide strip just in from edge of zipper tape.

Double-slide zipper

Regular zipper

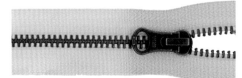

★ Please attach zipper in the most convenient direction, whether that is the right or left.

Installing Zipper: Simple Method

Apply glue to outside of zipper slot.

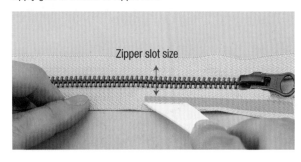

Zipper slot size

Press end and gently adhere to body.

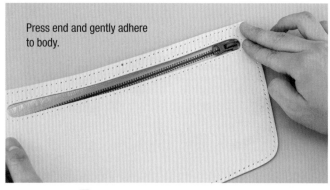

After gluing

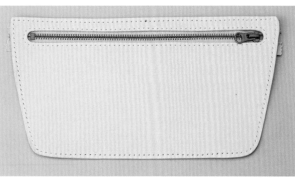

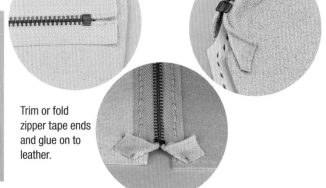

Trim or fold zipper tape ends and glue on to leather.

Installing Zipper after Marking Positions

1 Add guidelines or markings to prevent distortion. Draw thin lines with a hard graphite pencil, for example.

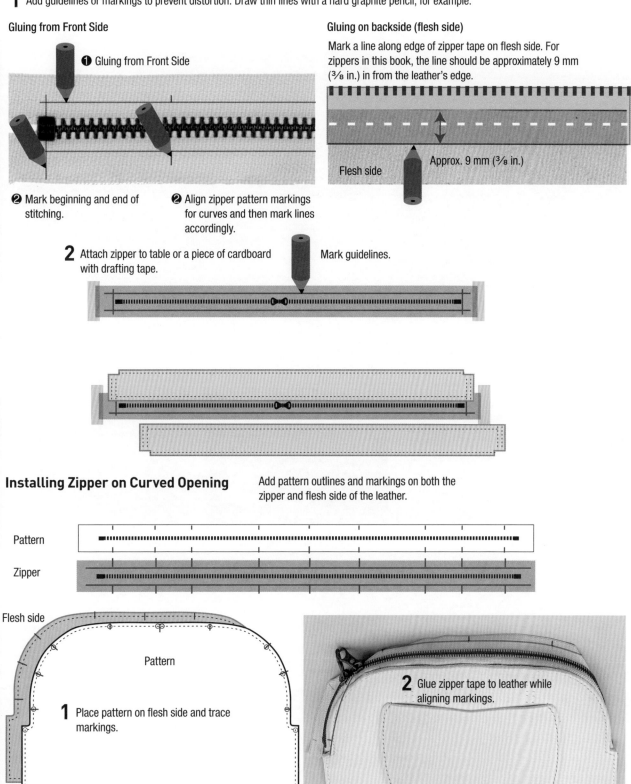

Gluing from Front Side

❶ Gluing from Front Side

❷ Mark beginning and end of stitching.

❷ Align zipper pattern markings for curves and then mark lines accordingly.

Gluing on backside (flesh side)

Mark a line along edge of zipper tape on flesh side. For zippers in this book, the line should be approximately 9 mm (³⁄₈ in.) in from the leather's edge.

Flesh side

Approx. 9 mm (³⁄₈ in.)

2 Attach zipper to table or a piece of cardboard with drafting tape.

Mark guidelines.

Installing Zipper on Curved Opening

Add pattern outlines and markings on both the zipper and flesh side of the leather.

Pattern

Zipper

Flesh side

Pattern

1 Place pattern on flesh side and trace markings.

2 Glue zipper tape to leather while aligning markings.

Three-Dimensional Bonding

The key is to stretch the seam allowance on the gusset side and align it with the curve of the body's seam allowance.

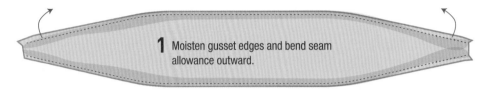

1 Moisten gusset edges and bend seam allowance outward.

Center

2 Apply Bond G Clear along seam allowances of body and gusset. Let dry for a few minutes. Then proceed to bond together while sandwiching paper between the pieces. Be sure to align the central stitching holes.

Details

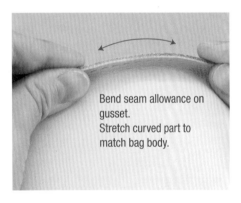

Bend seam allowance on gusset.
Stretch curved part to match bag body.

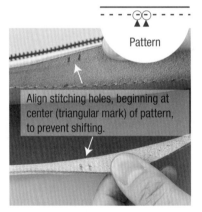

Pattern

Align stitching holes, beginning at center (triangular mark) of pattern, to prevent shifting.

Use needles to stabilize.

3 Temporarily stitch to prevent adhesive from peeling off and stitching holes from shifting.

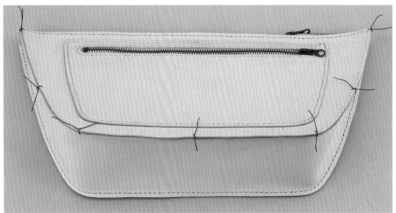

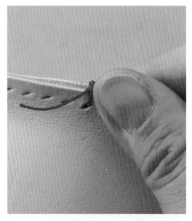

Stitching Turned Edges

This is an advanced stitching method. The key is to firmly open the stitching holes so that it's easier to pass the needle through from the inside.

1 When fitting to a curved surface, moisten and bend seam allowance of the underside leather.

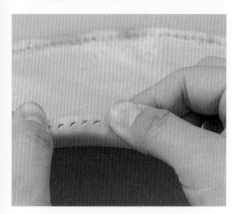

2 Apply Bond G Clear to seam allowance on both leather pieces.

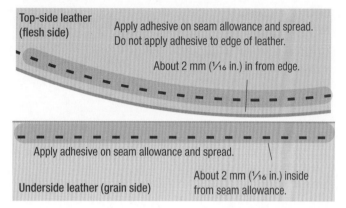

Top-side leather (flesh side) Apply adhesive on seam allowance and spread. Do not apply adhesive to edge of leather.

About 2 mm (1/16 in.) in from edge.

Apply adhesive on seam allowance and spread.

Underside leather (grain side) About 2 mm (1/16 in.) inside from seam allowance.

3 Proceed to bond while aligning seam holes with paper sandwiched between leather pieces. Temporarily secure with stitches to prevent adhesive from peeling off or seam holes from shifting.

After bonding, widen stitching holes by poking each one with a scratch awl. This will make stitching easier.

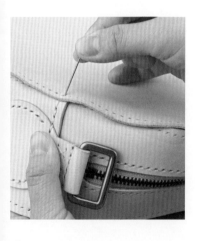

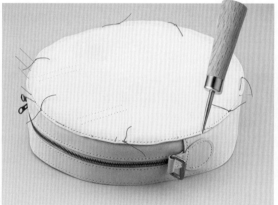

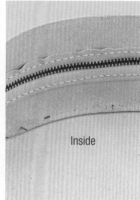

Inside

4 Stitch while firmly holding leather pieces both on inside and outside with your hands.

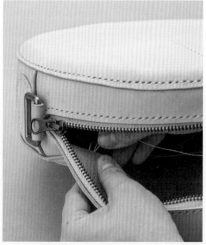

Modifying Pattern Size on Main Components

Alter patterns so that stitching holes are even. While it's easy to alter the length of straight sections of the pattern, it's not recommended for areas with curves, since it can be quite challenging.

Basic Size Modification

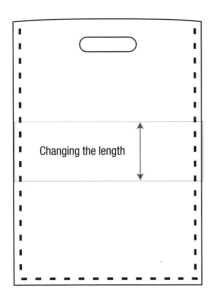

Changing the length

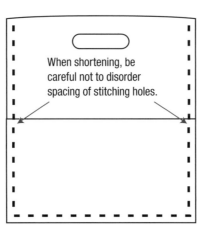

When shortening, be careful not to disorder spacing of stitching holes.

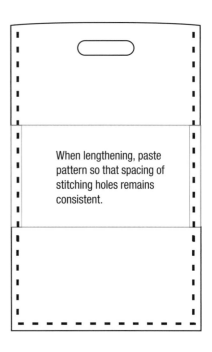

When lengthening, paste pattern so that spacing of stitching holes remains consistent.

Bag with Side Gusse   Illustrated with a simple tote bag as an example.

★ For easier understanding, the patterns are connected.

Changing bag depth

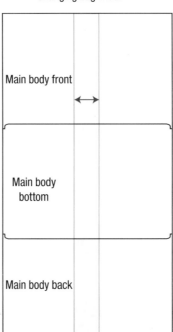

Main body front

Main body bottom

Main body back

Main body side

Changing bag width

Main body front

Main body bottom

Main body back

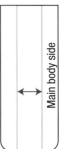

Main body side

Always alter size within the area enclosed in straight lines.

Bag with Four-Sided Gussets

Diagram uses a backpack: briefcase type

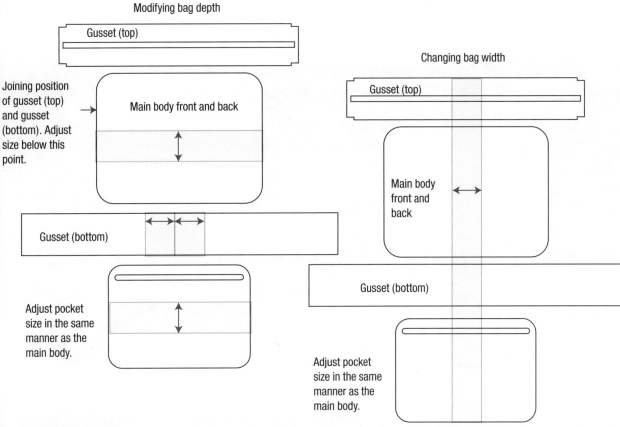

Modifying bag depth

Gusset (top)

Joining position of gusset (top) and gusset (bottom). Adjust size below this point.

Main body front and back

Changing bag width

Gusset (top)

Gusset (bottom)

Main body front and back

Adjust pocket size in the same manner as the main body.

Gusset (bottom)

Adjust pocket size in the same manner as the main body.

Installing Hardware

★ When not changing hardware size.

Cut out handle pattern and install hardware while adjusting the position.
Ensure equal spacing between left and right handles.

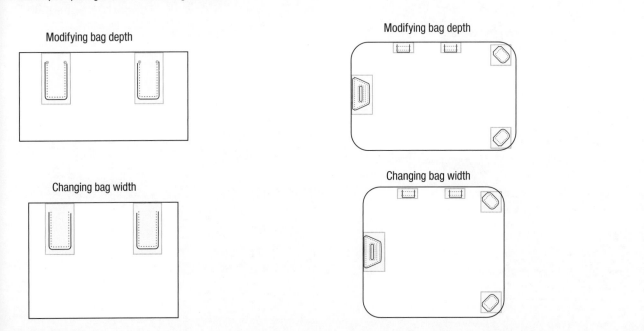

Modifying bag depth

Modifying bag depth

Changing bag width

Changing bag width

Adding Pockets

In this book, to minimize the number of parts, attached pockets are kept to a minimum. Customize the design provided here to suit your preference.

Adding External Pockets

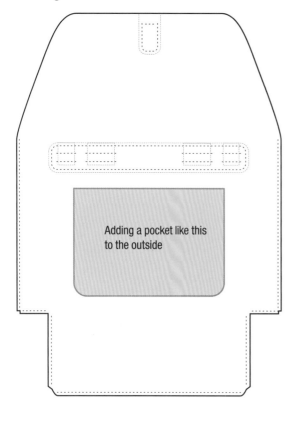

Adding a pocket like this to the outside

1 Cut leather for pocket.

2 Place one prong from a two-prong lacing chisel against leather edge to mark seam.
(You can mark line about 4 mm [⅛ in.] inside from leather edge.)

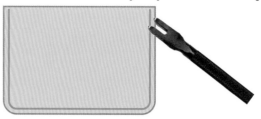

3 Punch stitching holes along the marked line with a lacing chisel.

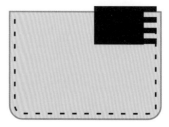

For punching stitching holes at pocket mouth, adjust position of four-prong lacing chisel so that one hole is punched just outside the pocket.

4 Apply adhesive to pocket seam allowance and bond to main body.
5 Align prongs of four-prong lacing chisel with punched stitching holes of pocket punched in step 3. Firmly punch stitching holes to main body.

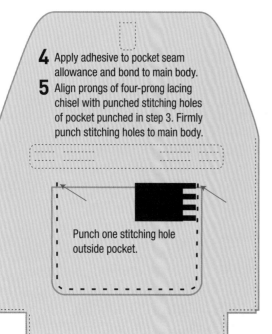

Punch one stitching hole outside pocket.

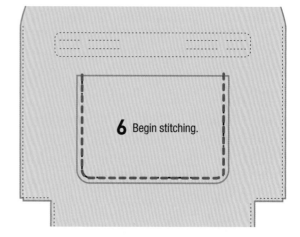

6 Begin stitching.

Adding Inner Pockets

To minimize visible stitches on outer surface, sew only pocket opening.

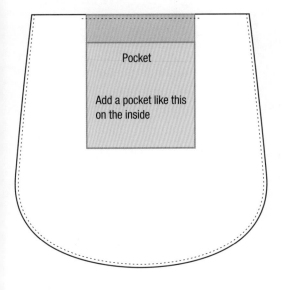

Pocket

Add a pocket like this on the inside

1 Cut leather for pocket.

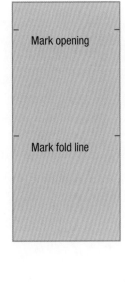

Mark opening

Mark fold line

2 Place one prong of two-prong lacing chisel against leather edge to mark seam.

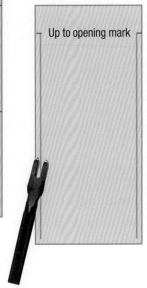

Up to opening mark

3 Punch stitching holes along marked line, up to about 5 mm (⅛ in.) before the fold line, with a lacing chisel.

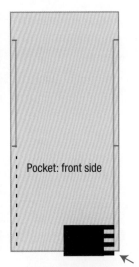

Pocket: front side

Punch stitching holes so that one hole ends up just outside the pocket.

4 Fold pocket and apply glue to seam allowance. Align four-prong lacing chisel with the stitching holes opened in step 3, and firmly punch stitching holes through front and rear flap of pocket .

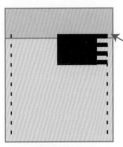

Stitching holes at the opening should protrude one prong width.

5 Use two-pronged lacing chisel to mark seam allowance line. Punch stitching holes along marked line of pocket flap to sew onto main body.

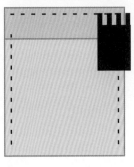

6 Sew pocket sides.

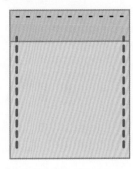

7 Align edge with main body and glue. Align pocket flap with stitching holes punched in step 5, and punch stitching holes into main body.

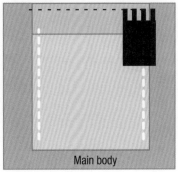

Main body

8 Begin stitching.

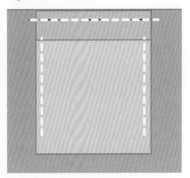

Zipper Pull Tab

Attaching a pull tab makes it easier to open and close the zipper.
Can also be attached after completing project.

Pull Tab Pattern
100%
one piece for
each side

1 Punch stitching holes, cut leather, and apply burnishing agent to both the surface and edge.

2 Align with stitching holes at zipper end. Bond together and stitch.

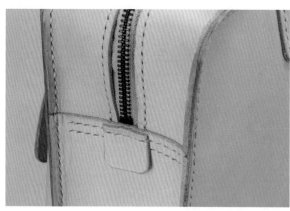

Adding Length to the Shoulder Strap (if desired after completion)

Strap Connector Pattern   100%
one piece for each end

For 24 mm (1 in.) wide strap

For 30 mm (1¼ in.) wide strap

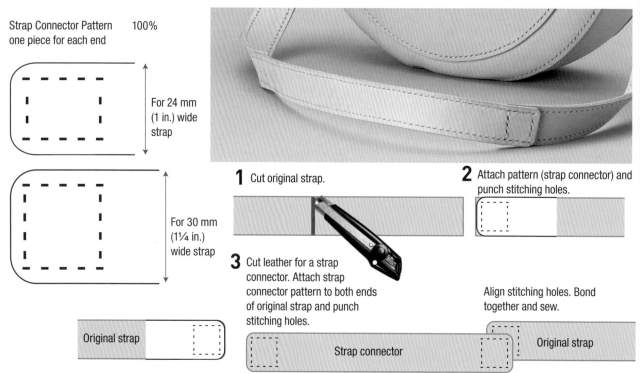

1 Cut original strap.

2 Attach pattern (strap connector) and punch stitching holes.

3 Cut leather for a strap connector. Attach strap connector pattern to both ends of original strap and punch stitching holes.

Align stitching holes. Bond together and sew.

Original strap

Strap connector

Original strap

Stitching Three Pieces of Leather, or More, at Once

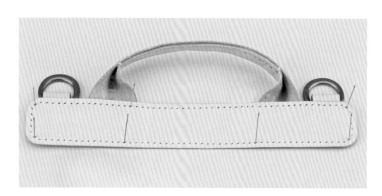

It's important to firmly punch stitching holes so that the needle can pass through without much effort. After bonding, widen the stitching holes a bit—one by one—while aligning them with a scratch awl. This makes it easier to sew.

When Stitching Holes Don't Align

Sometimes, even if you try to align the stitching holes as you progress, the number of holes will no longer match. Vegetable-tanned leather can stretch to some extent, so you can adjust by using the following method. Just moisten and stretch the leather to fit.

Peeling Off Glued Area

Insert scratch awl into gap in glued edge. Move scratch awl at an angle and peel off.

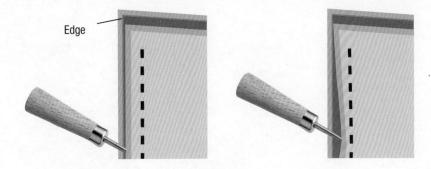

Edge

When Openings Do Not Align

If you can't align the opening, peel about 10 cm (4 in.) of the glued seam allowance back from the opening. Moisten and stretch the shorter piece of leather, then, when dry, add necessary holes with a lacing needle.

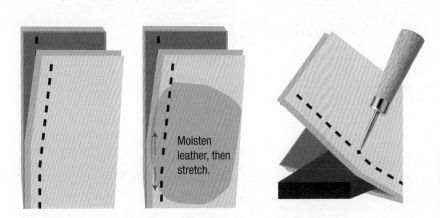

Moisten leather, then stretch.

Stitching While Aligning the Holes

Stop a few stitches before the added hole. Then, resume stitching from the opening as you adjust hole positions, using a scratch awl.

Once stitching is complete, open the joined seam and apply glue. Then bond securely.

Stitch Doesn't Align at Middle

Similar to adjusting an opening, moisten the leather to stretch, then add a hole and stitch.

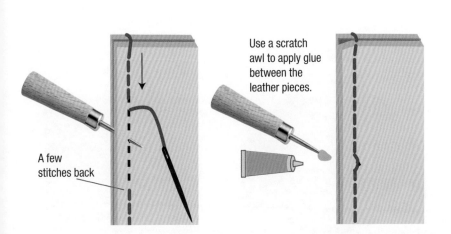

A few stitches back

Use a scratch awl to apply glue between the leather pieces.

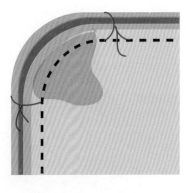

Using Oil-Tanned Leather

Light-beige leather bags dramatically change when using colored leather, even if they are the same design.

Images of tanned leather bags in this book have been digitally colored for illustration.

Although tanned, this type of leather is actually softer than natural vegetable-tanned leather because it is suffused with a healthy amount of oil. Similar to natural vegetable-tanned leather, oil-tanned leather is suitable for making hand-stitched leather products. In addition, production steps are the same for both types of leather.

There are many colors available.
In this book, all stitching threads are white, but you can also enjoy variations by using threads in similar colors or using complementary colors to accentuate the stitches.

The main advantage of dyed leather is that it hides scratches, color variations, sunburn, etc. In other words, it is more worry-free.

It is safe to apply Leather Fix to colored leather before sewing. This will prevent color transfer and stop color from being rubbed off as well.

If you wish to use a dark-colored and light-colored piece of leather, be sure to wet the edges and test for color transfer with a piece of paper towel. Avoid different colors if you find any transfer.

Chapter 3

Instructions for Making Various Bags

In this chapter, we introduce structural and production variations for bags with various designs.

Please refer to chapter 1, "Basic Procedures," for initial production.
Any references to chapter 2, "Practical Application of Basic Techniques," will be indicated within a black border.

Leather and Hardware Used

All vegetable-tanned leather is approximately 2 mm (1/16 in.) thick. The hardware is made mostly of brass.

Size Specification

Bag sizes include a 4 mm (1/8 in.) seam allowance, so interior dimensions will be slightly smaller.
Additionally, the actual size may vary depending on contents.
Approximate bag sizes for individuals with heights of 175 cm (68⅞ in.) and 165 cm (65 in.) can serve as a rough guide.

Instructions Page

Diagrams are depicted with thicker lines for easier understanding, since they have been reduced.
Stitching hole numbers may differ between the diagram and the actual item.

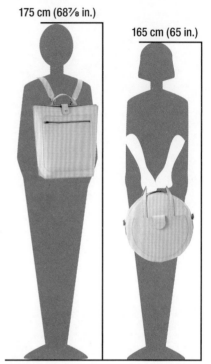

175 cm (68⅞ in.)

165 cm (65 in.)

Pattern

Provided at a 50% reduction.
Use a 200% enlargement. ★ Pages 66 and 120–121 are enlarged 210%.
Please refer to pages concerning patterns in chapter 1, "Basic Procedures."
Hardware found in each pattern has also been scaled down by the same ratio. There may be some margin of error because of each bag's three-dimensional nature.

Brass Hardware

Similar to leather that browns due to aging, brass hardware may develop rust, but this just adds character.
Initially, care must be taken, since vegetable-tanned leather is milky white and rust may be more noticeable in this state. That being said, it is best to cover the hardware with tissue paper, or something similar, to protect it from transferring rust to the leather during storage.

Front

Size

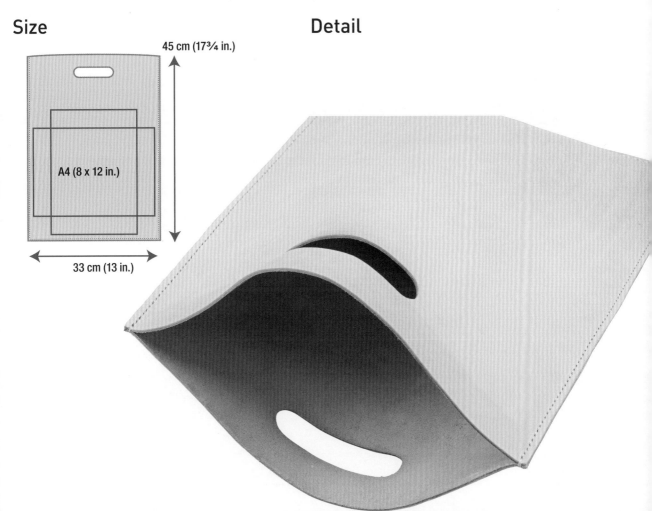

A4 (8 x 12 in.)

45 cm (17¾ in.)

33 cm (13 in.)

Detail

Patterns

Photocopy enlargement scale: 210%

Main body front and back: 2 pieces

How To: Main body front and back

Punching Stitching Holes and Cutting Leather

- Apply burnishing agent to flesh side and edges marked with red lines.
- Mark positions of ○, found on the pattern, on flesh side of leather.

Creating the Main Body

Align stitching holes.
Then glue and stitch.

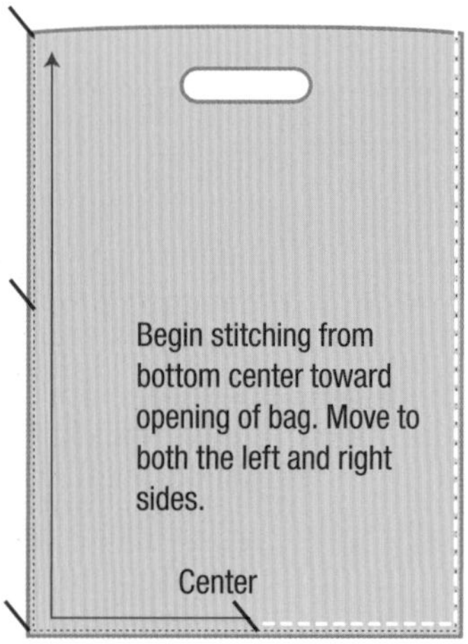

Begin stitching from bottom center toward opening of bag. Move to both the left and right sides.

Center

Apply burnishing agent along edges after stitching together.

Securing with Double-Sided Tape

Use double-sided tape to bond leather pieces along seam allowance on areas that are flat and consist mainly of straight lines.
Use double-sided tape that is about 2 mm (1/16 in.) narrower than seam allowance width.

1 Attach tape on flesh side along seam allowance.

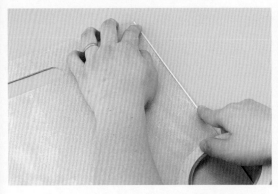
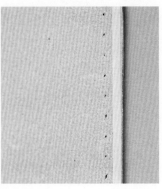

2 Use needles to align marked stitching holes and bond leather pieces while peeling release liner on double-sided tape.

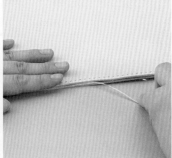

3 Double-sided tape bonding strength is weaker than that of contact glue. Be sure to secure leather with clips, or tie it with thread in several places, to prevent it from peeling off before stitching.

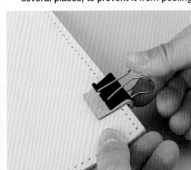

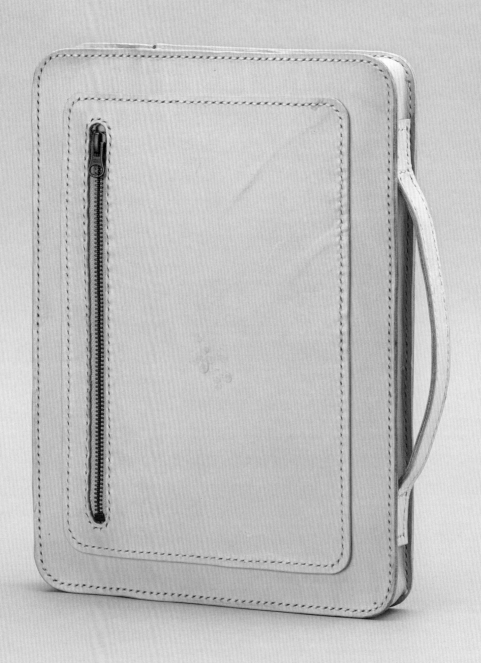

Front

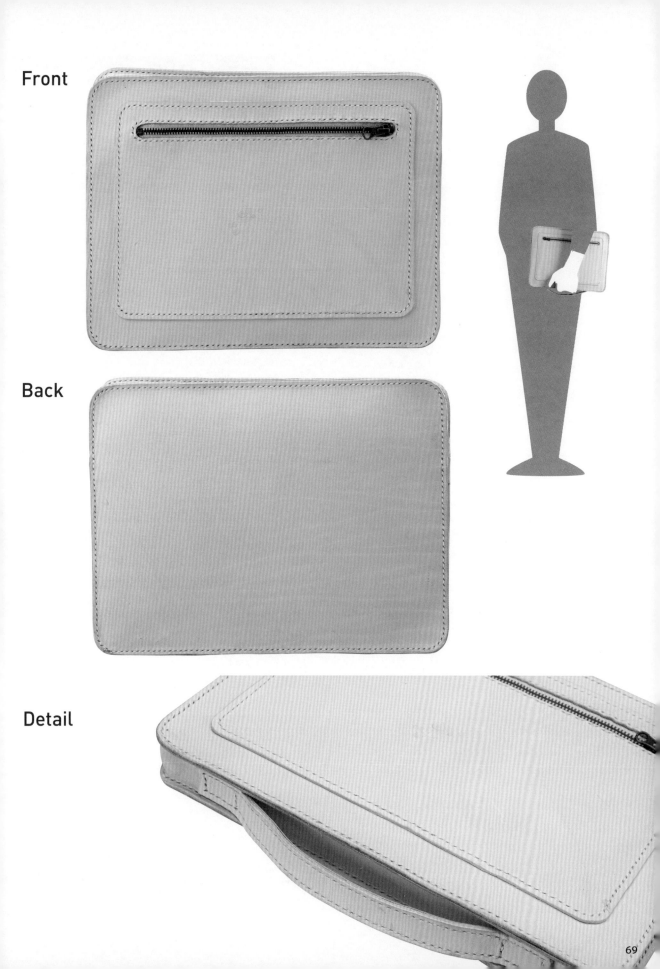

Back

Detail

How To:

Punching Stitching Holes and Cutting Leather

See "Creating a Simple Handle," p. 40–45.
Two-ply and stitched along the edges.
See "Installing a Zipper," p. 50–51.
See "Three-Dimensional Bonding," p. 52.
See "Stitching Three Pieces of Leather, or More, at Once," p. 58.

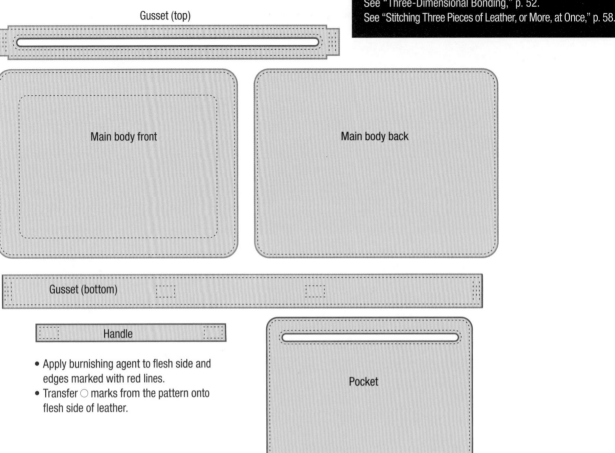

Gusset (top)

Main body front

Main body back

Gusset (bottom)

Handle

Pocket

- Apply burnishing agent to flesh side and edges marked with red lines.
- Transfer ○ marks from the pattern onto flesh side of leather.

Creating Parts and Attaching to Main Body

1 Install zipper on pocket.

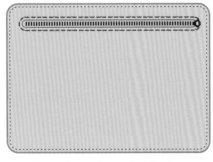

★ Please choose zipper orientation for easy opening.

2 Align stitching holes, glue pocket on main body front, and then sew on.

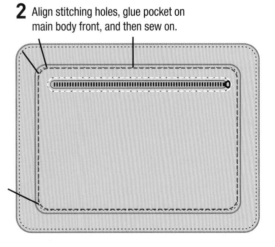

3 Make handle.
If stitching is involved, stitch all areas except those that will be used to attach to the main body.

4 Adding zipper to gusset (top).

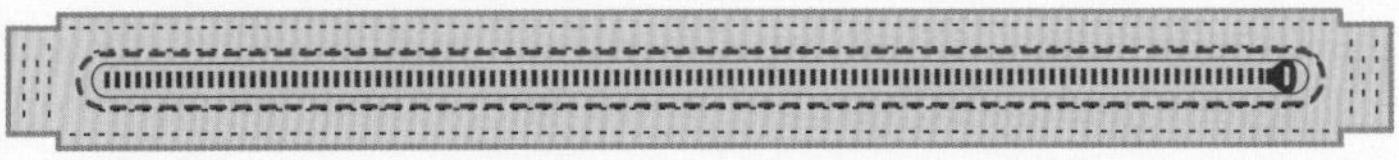

5 Align stitching holes and bond handle to gusset (bottom).

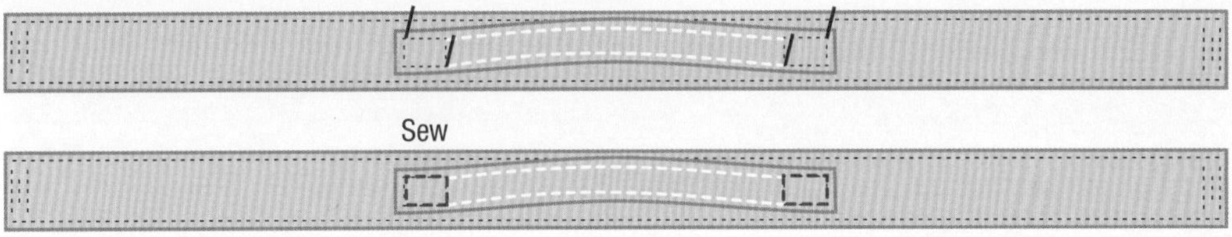

Sew

6 Align stitching holes and bond both gussets (top and bottom).

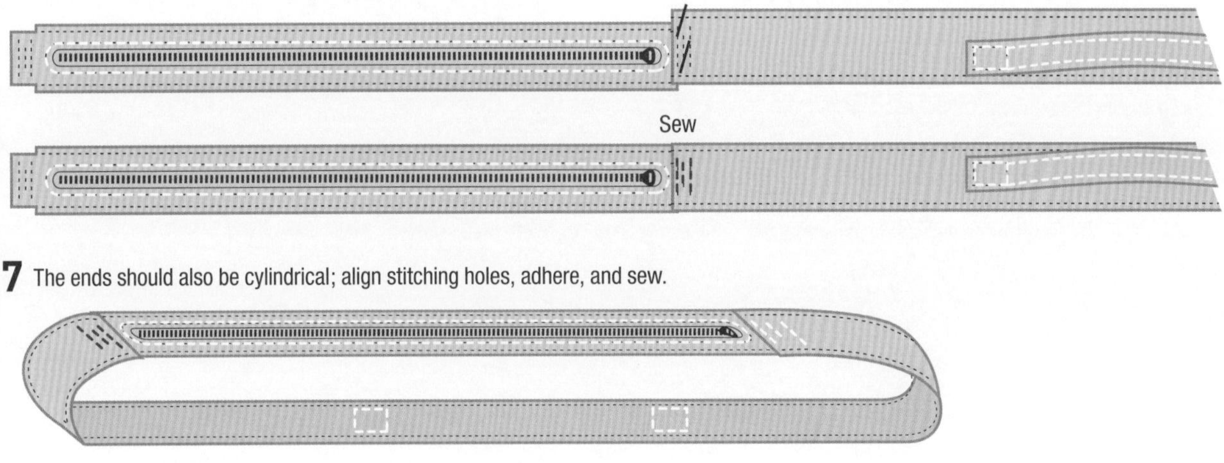

Sew

7 The ends should also be cylindrical; align stitching holes, adhere, and sew.

Creating Main Body

1 Moisten and bend gusset seam allowance.

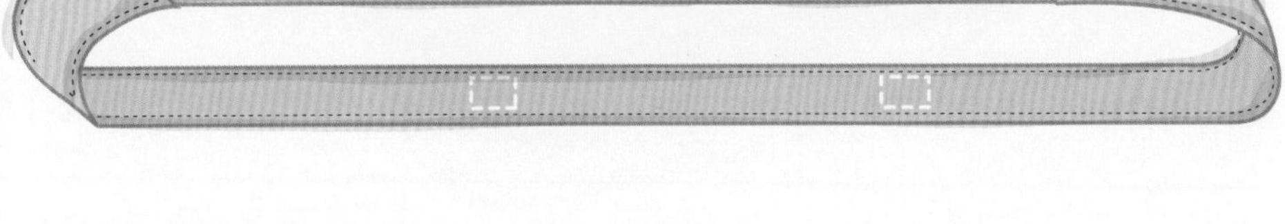

2 Glue gusset to main body back. Align stitching holes and temporarily secure working piece in place to prevent shifting.

★ Ensure that zipper direction is the same as that of the pocket.

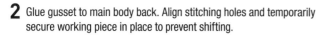

Sew

3 Glue gusset to main body front. Align stitching holes, and temporarily secure working piece in place to prevent shifting.

Sew

Patterns

Photocopy enlargement
scale: 200%

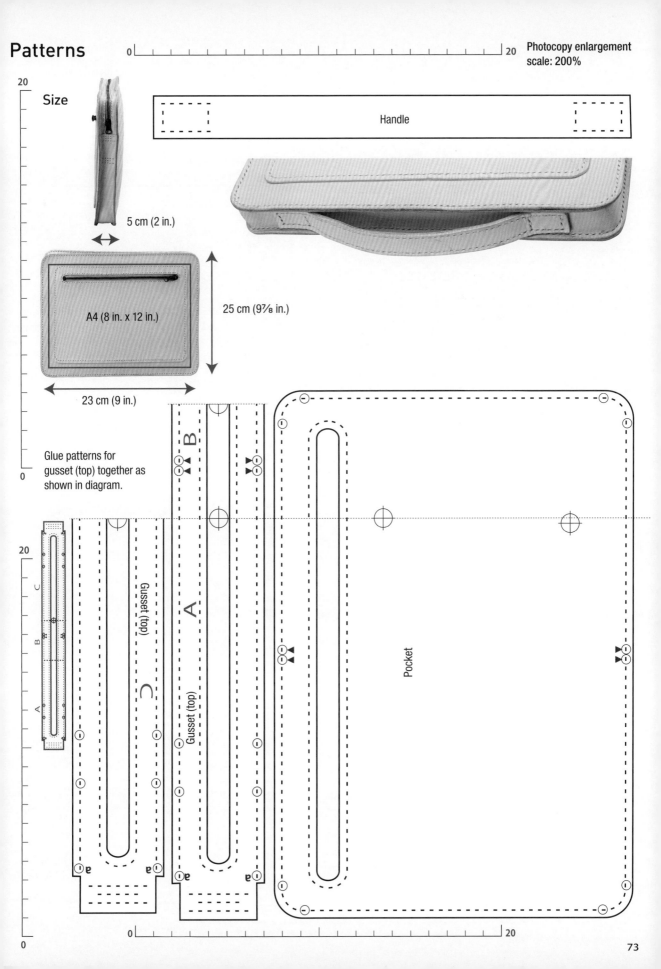

Size

5 cm (2 in.)

A4 (8 in. x 12 in.)

25 cm (9⅞ in.)

23 cm (9 in.)

Handle

Glue patterns for gusset (top) together as shown in diagram.

B

A

C

Gusset (top)

Gusset (top)

C

B

A

Pocket

Patterns

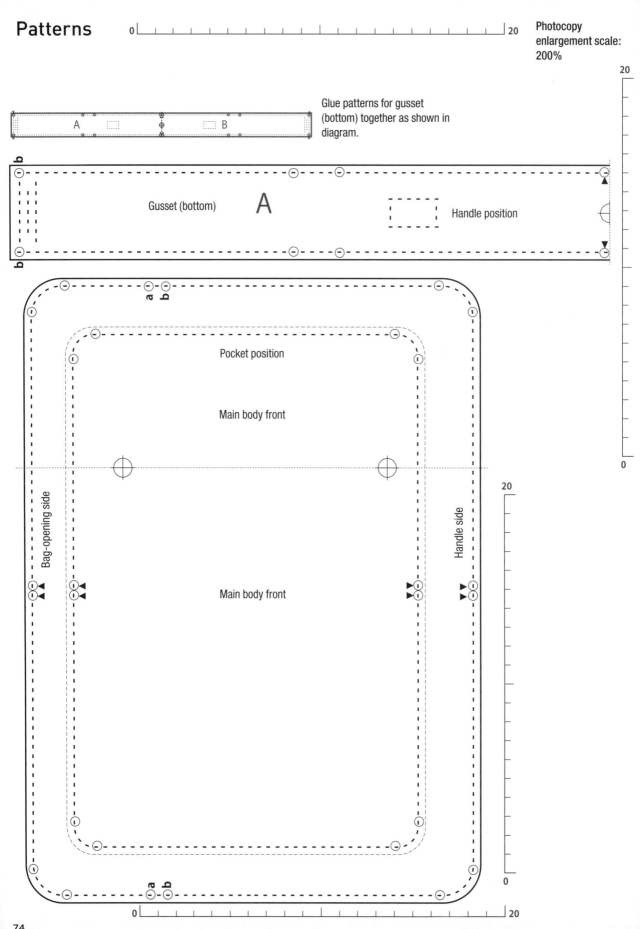

0 |_____| 20

Photocopy enlargement scale: 200%

Glue patterns for gusset (bottom) together as shown in diagram.

A   B

Gusset (bottom)   A   Handle position

Pocket position

Main body front

Bag-opening side

Handle side

Main body front

Patterns

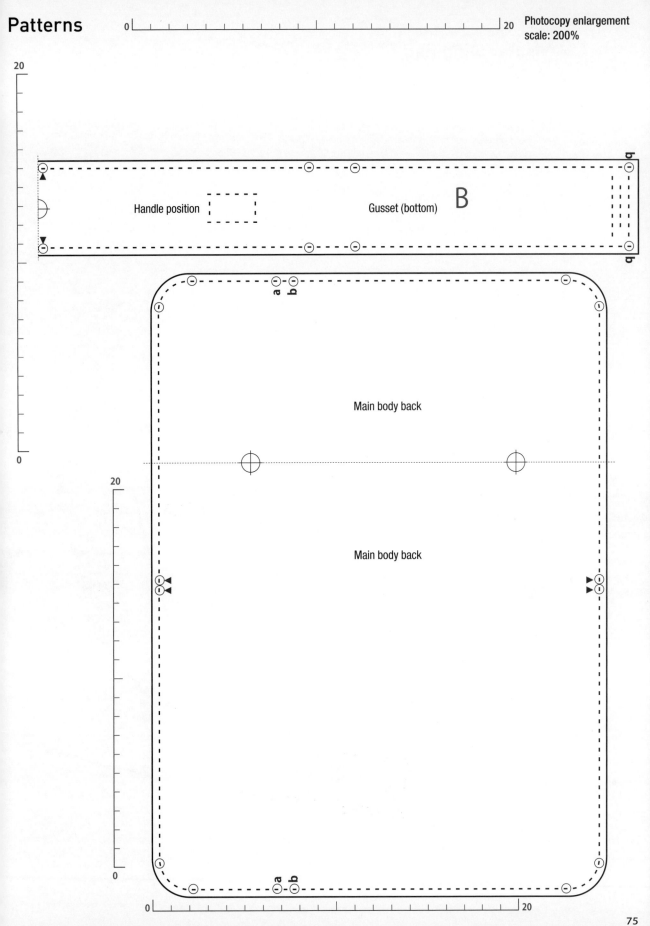

Handle position

Gusset (bottom)

B

Main body back

Main body back

Tanned Leather Bag No. 4
Navicular Sling Bag

Front

Back

Side

Detail

How To:

Punching Stitching Holes and Cutting Leather

See "How to Make Shoulder Strap and Pattern," p. 40–47.
Stitched along edges.
See "Installing a Zipper," p. 50–51.
See "Three-Dimensional Bonding," p. 52.

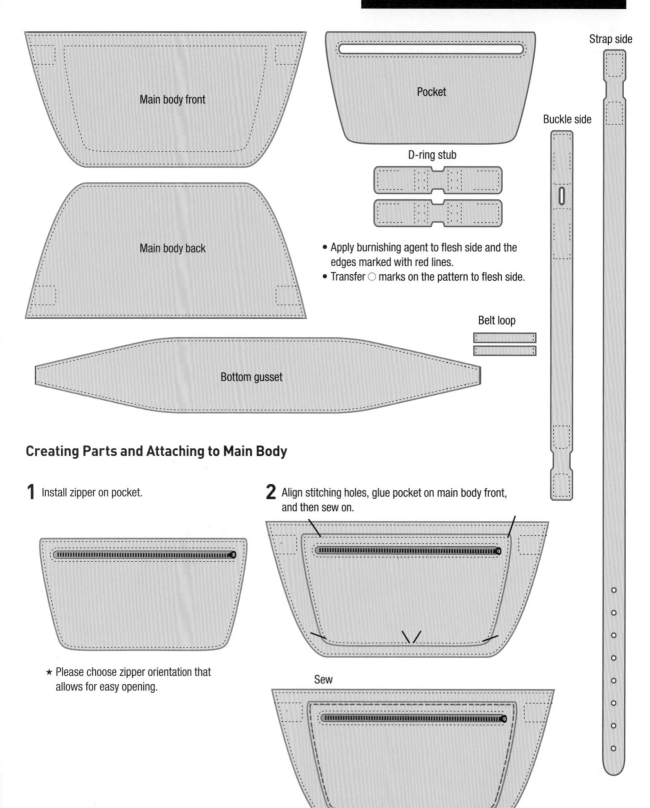

Main body front

Pocket

D-ring stub

Main body back

- Apply burnishing agent to flesh side and the edges marked with red lines.
- Transfer ○ marks on the pattern to flesh side.

Belt loop

Bottom gusset

Strap side

Buckle side

Creating Parts and Attaching to Main Body

1 Install zipper on pocket.

★ Please choose zipper orientation that allows for easy opening.

2 Align stitching holes, glue pocket on main body front, and then sew on.

Sew

Creating the Main Body

1 Install zipper to main body front and back.

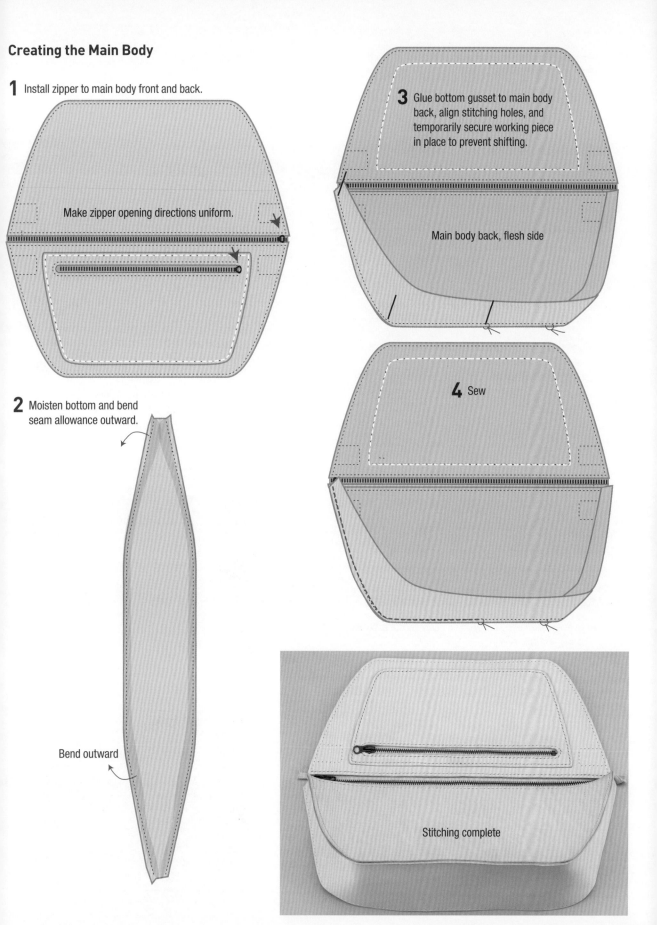

Make zipper opening directions uniform.

2 Moisten bottom and bend seam allowance outward.

Bend outward

3 Glue bottom gusset to main body back, align stitching holes, and temporarily secure working piece in place to prevent shifting.

Main body back, flesh side

4 Sew

Stitching complete

5 Moisten bottom gusset and bend seam allowance outward. To align main body front, stretch and bend seam allowance.

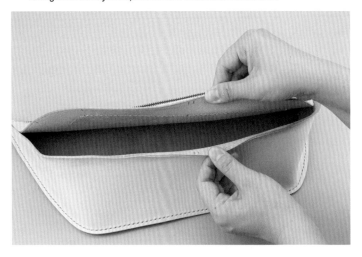

Sandwich a piece of paper between the leather pieces. Glue while aligning the stitching holes.

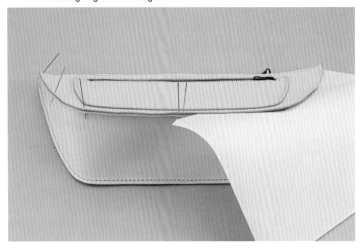

Align seam allowances firmly, temporarily secure to prevent slippage, and then sew.

6 Moisten D-ring stub.

Insert D-ring, align stitching holes, glue, and sew.

Stitching complete

Wrap D-ring stub around main body and glue while aligning stitching holes.

Sew

Patterns

Photocopy enlargement
scale: 200%

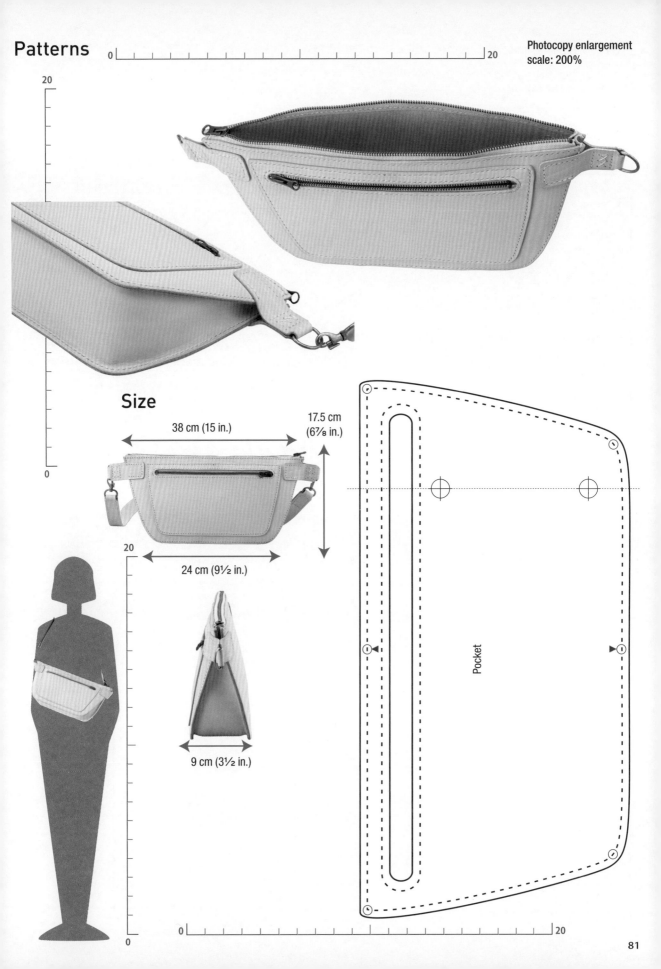

Size

38 cm (15 in.)

17.5 cm
(6⅞ in.)

24 cm (9½ in.)

9 cm (3½ in.)

Pocket

Patterns

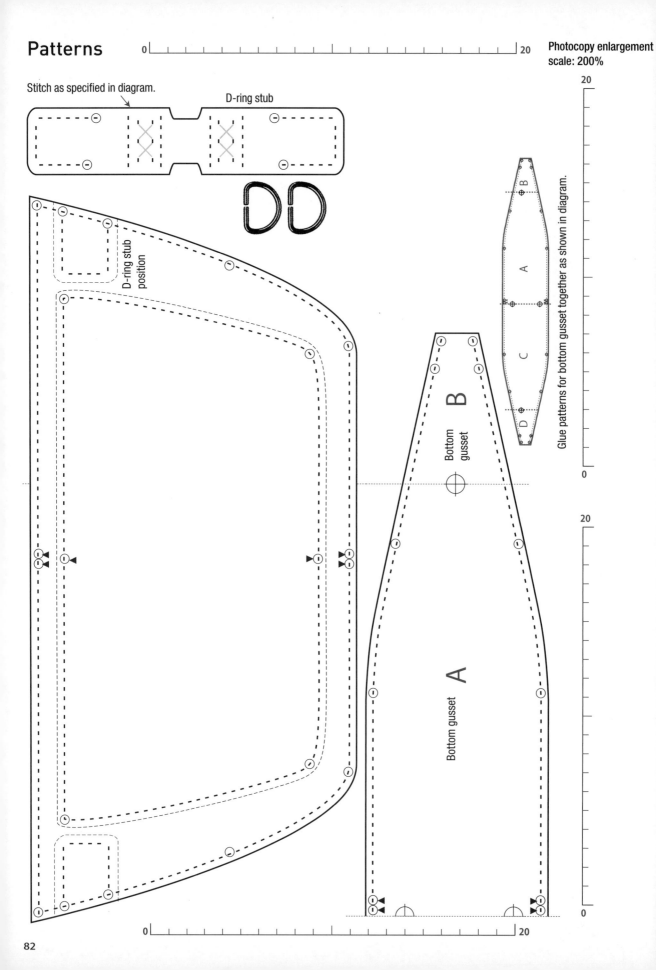

Stitch as specified in diagram.

D-ring stub

D-ring stub position

Bottom gusset

B

Bottom gusset

A

Glue patterns for bottom gusset together as shown in diagram.

Photocopy enlargement scale: 200%

Patterns

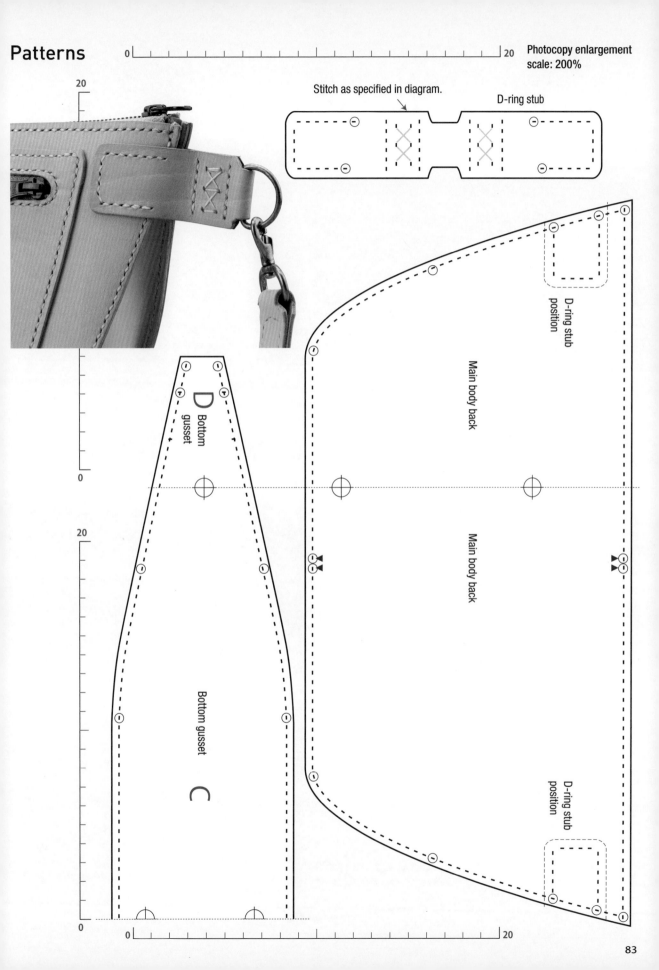

Stitch as specified in diagram.

D-ring stub

D-ring stub position

Main body back

Main body back

D-ring stub position

D Bottom gusset

Bottom gusset

C

Boxy Sling Bag

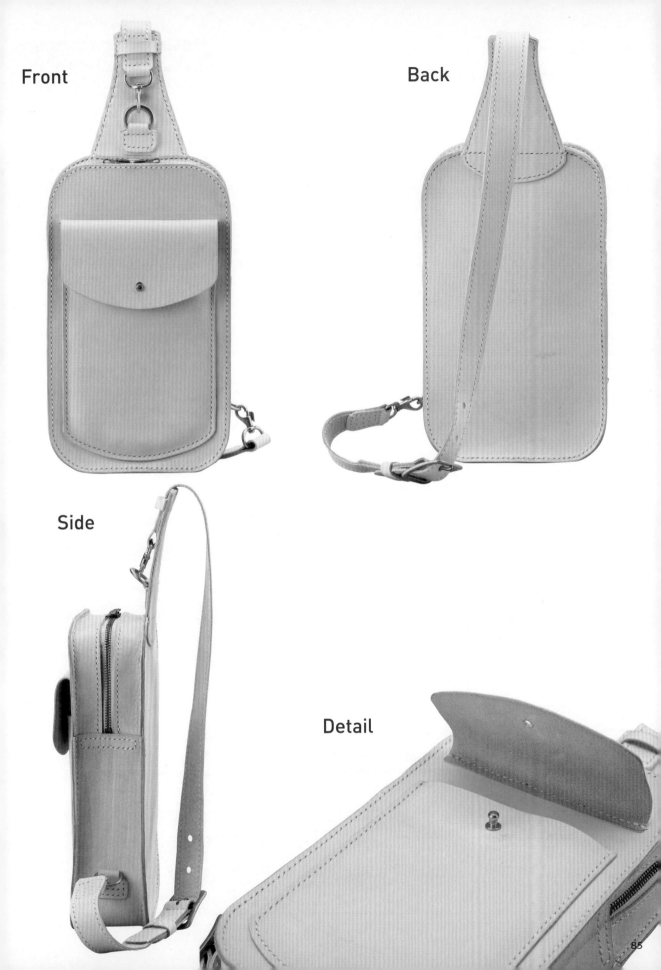

Front

Back

Side

Detail

85

How To:

Punching Stitching Holes and Cutting Leather

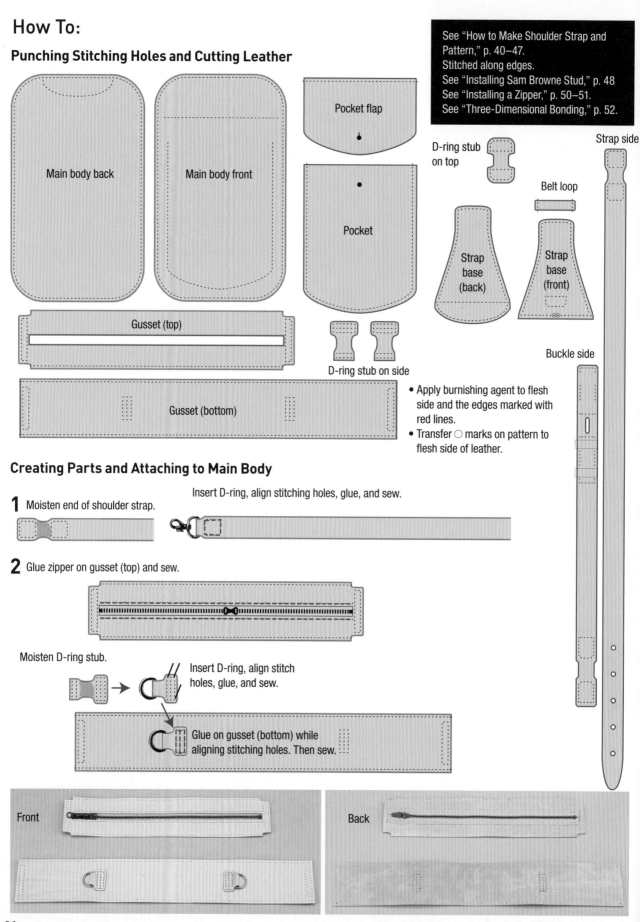

See "How to Make Shoulder Strap and Pattern," p. 40–47.
Stitched along edges.
See "Installing Sam Browne Stud," p. 48
See "Installing a Zipper," p. 50–51.
See "Three-Dimensional Bonding," p. 52.

Main body back

Main body front

Pocket flap

Pocket

D-ring stub on top

Strap side

Belt loop

Strap base (back)

Strap base (front)

Gusset (top)

D-ring stub on side

Buckle side

Gusset (bottom)

- Apply burnishing agent to flesh side and the edges marked with red lines.
- Transfer ○ marks on pattern to flesh side of leather.

Creating Parts and Attaching to Main Body

1 Moisten end of shoulder strap.

Insert D-ring, align stitching holes, glue, and sew.

2 Glue zipper on gusset (top) and sew.

Moisten D-ring stub.

Insert D-ring, align stitch holes, glue, and sew.

Glue on gusset (bottom) while aligning stitching holes. Then sew.

Front

Back

3 Install Sam Browne stud on pocket.

Attach a thin leather piece that is slightly larger than the stud base, to prevent scratching.

Flesh side

4 Align stitching holes, then glue pocket and pocket flap to main body front. Then, sew it on.

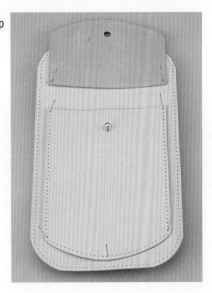

5 Attach belt loop on strap base (front).

Moisten D-ring stub (top) and insert D-ring. Then fold D-ring stub (top).

Align stitching holes. Then, glue and stitch.

6 Align stitching holes, then glue strap base (back) to main body back. Then, sew it on.

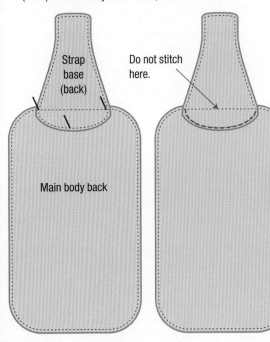

Strap base (back)

Do not stitch here.

Main body back

7 Glue belt loop on strap base (front) while aligning stitching holes. Then sew.

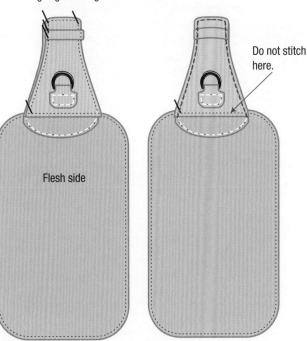

Do not stitch here.

Flesh side

Creating Main Body

1 Align stitching holes and bond gusset (top) and gusset (bottom).

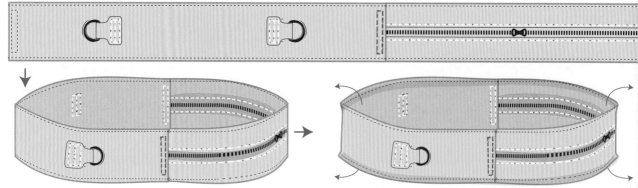

Moisten seam allowance and bend edges outward.

2 Glue gusset to main body back. Align stitching holes and temporarily secure working piece in place to prevent shifting.

3 Put main body front on working piece from step 2. Glue together while aligning stitching holes. Temporarily secure in place to prevent shifting.

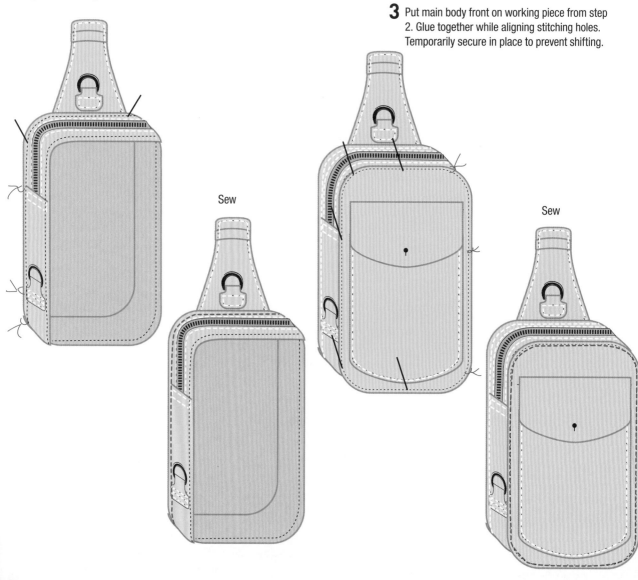

Sew

Sew

Patterns

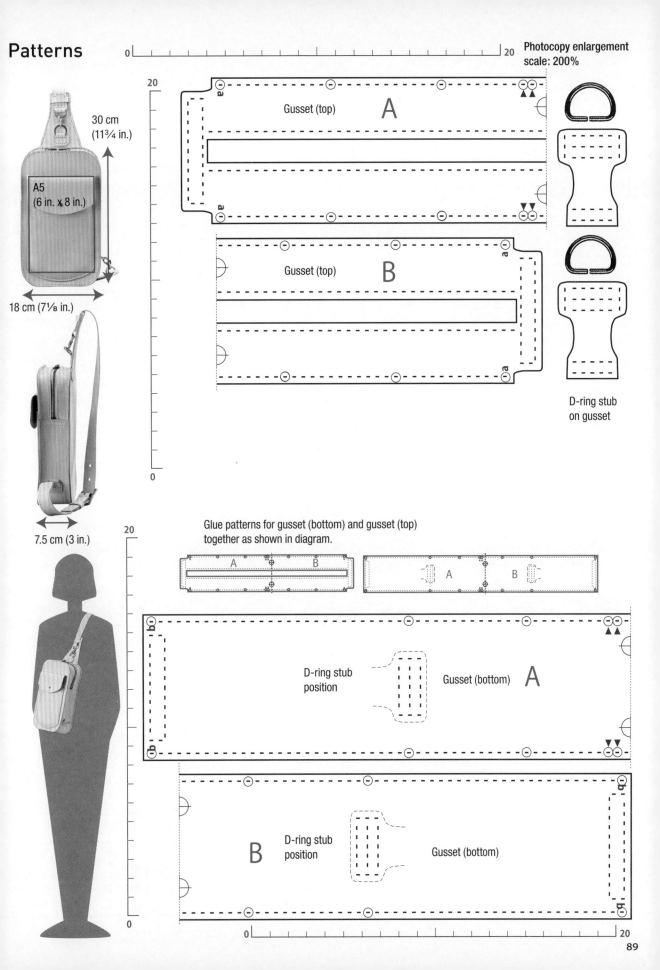

30 cm
(11¾ in.)

A5
(6 in. x 8 in.)

18 cm (7⅛ in.)

7.5 cm (3 in.)

Gusset (top)   A

Gusset (top)   B

D-ring stub
on gusset

Glue patterns for gusset (bottom) and gusset (top)
together as shown in diagram.

A   B

A   B

D-ring stub
position   Gusset (bottom)   A

D-ring stub
position   B   Gusset (bottom)

Patterns

0 |_____| 20

Photocopy enlargement
scale: 200%

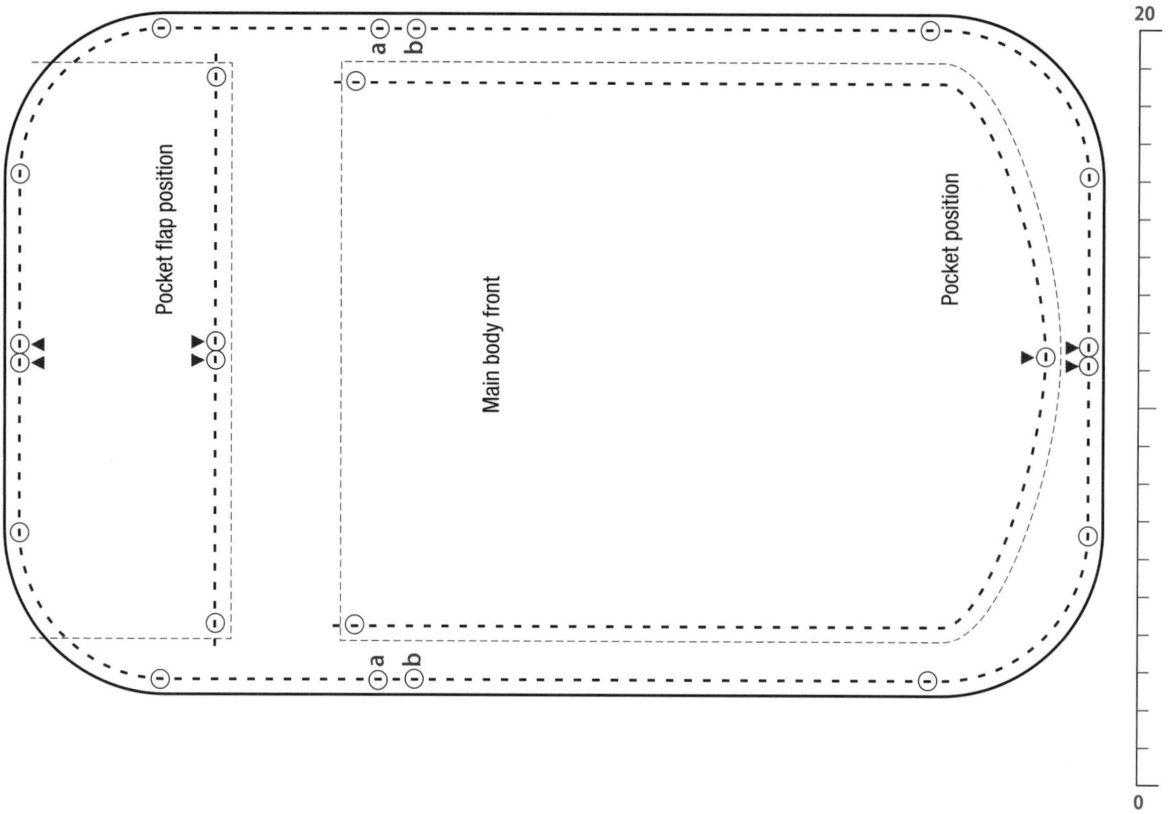

20

Pocket flap position

Main body front

Pocket position

a
b

a
b

0

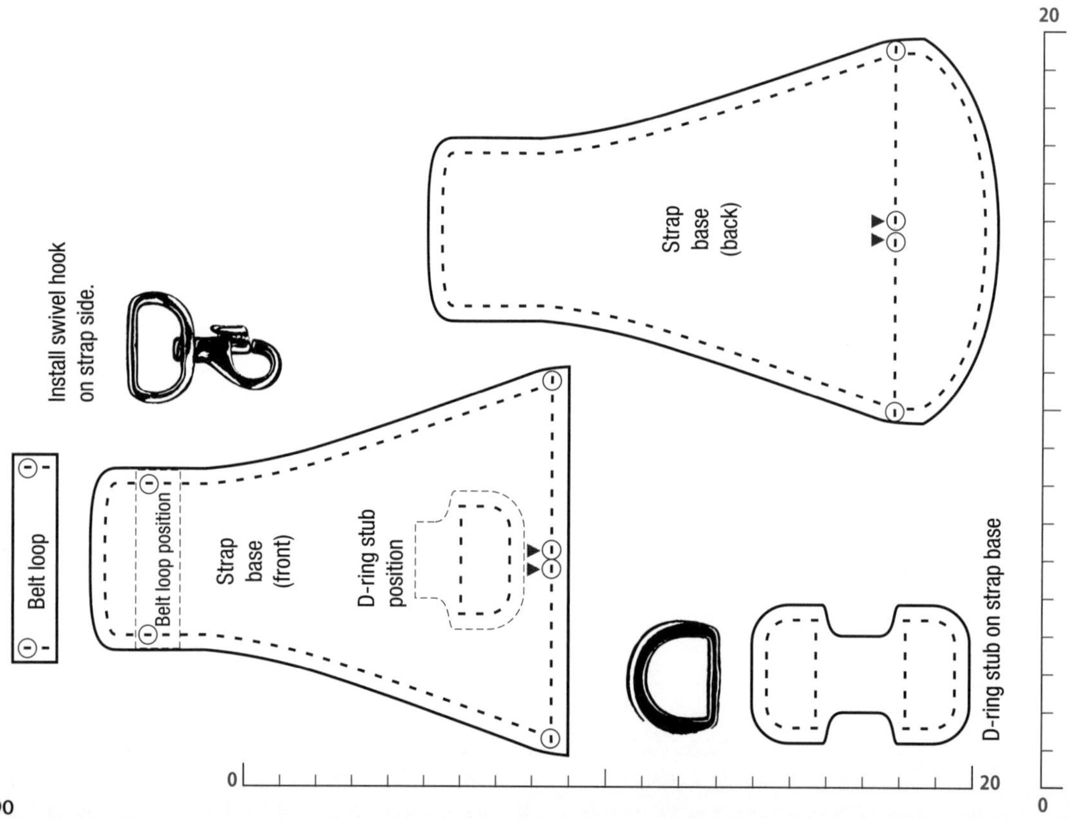

20

Install swivel hook
on strap side.

Strap
base
(back)

Belt loop

Strap
base
(front)

Belt loop position

D-ring stub
position

D-ring stub on strap base

0 |_____| 20

0

90

Patterns

Photocopy enlargement
scale: 200%

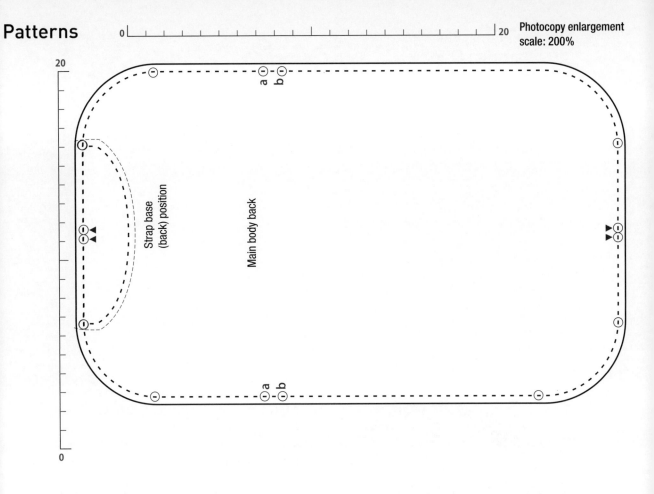

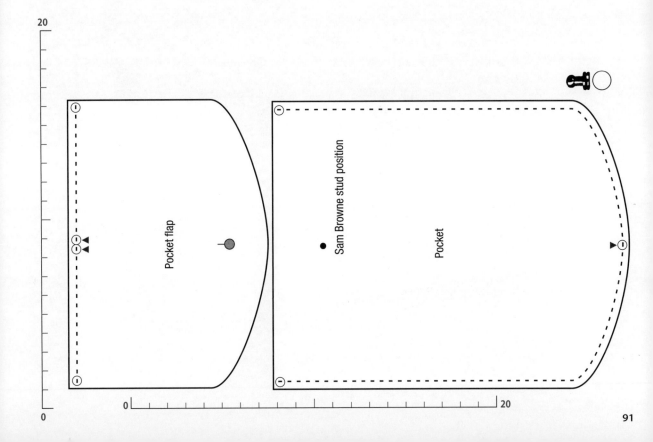

Tanned Leather Bag No. 6
Camera Bag

Front

Side

Back

Detail

Bicycle Bag

Attaching a belt to the back of this bag and mounting it on a bicycle may not work for certain bicycle models. Be sure to address any safety concerns on your own. The length of the belts for the handlebars or auxiliary strap, as well as the position of the auxiliary strap, may need adjustment.

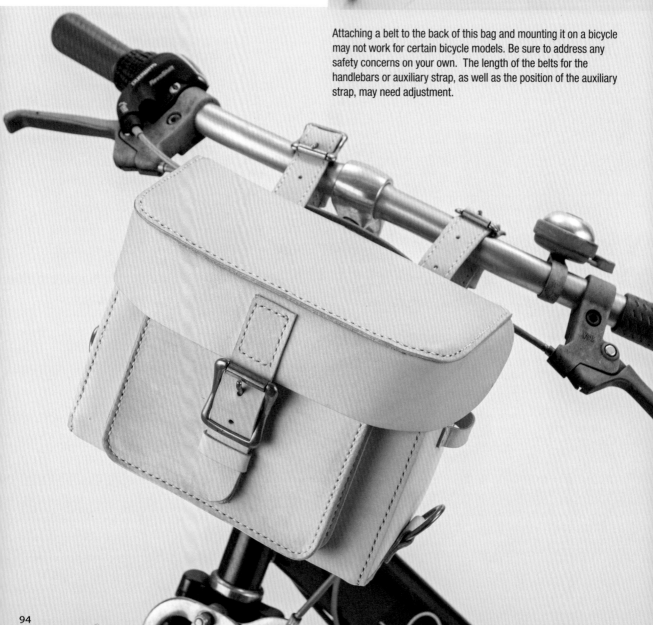

How To:

Punching Stitching Holes and Cutting Leather

See "How to Make Shoulder Strap and Pattern," p. 40–47.
Shoulder strap and handlebar straps are all stitched along edges.
See "Attaching Buckle" p. 46–47.
See "Stitching Turned Edges," p. 53.
See "Stitching Three Pieces of Leather, or More, at Once," p. 58.

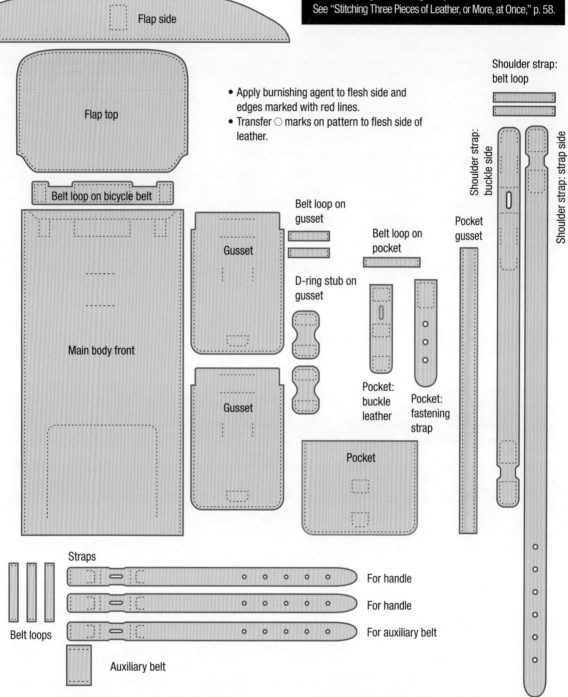

Flap side

Flap top

- Apply burnishing agent to flesh side and edges marked with red lines.
- Transfer ○ marks on pattern to flesh side of leather.

Shoulder strap: belt loop

Belt loop on bicycle belt

Belt loop on gusset

Belt loop on pocket

Shoulder strap: buckle side

Shoulder strap: strap side

Gusset

D-ring stub on gusset

Pocket gusset

Main body front

Pocket: buckle leather

Pocket: fastening strap

Gusset

Pocket

Straps

For handle

For handle

For auxiliary belt

Belt loops

Auxiliary belt

95

Creating Parts and Attaching to Main Body

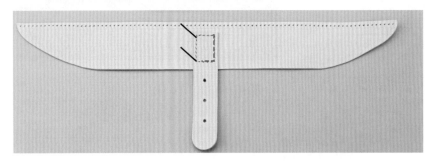

1 On flap side, glue on fastening strap and align stitching holes. Then sew.

2 Moisten top edge of flap side and bend inward.
Put flap top on flap side, glue them together, and align stitching holes. Then sew.

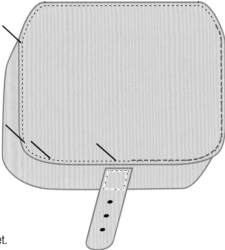

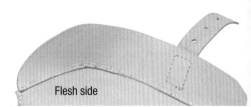

Flesh side

3 Attach buckle leather to pocket.

Fold belt loop.
Sew ends.

Insert buckle into buckle leather.

Pass through the belt loop. Then, glue buckle leather on pocket while aligning stitching holes and sew.

4 Glue pocket gusset on pocket while aligning stitching holes. Then, temporarily secure in place to prevent shifting. Sew.

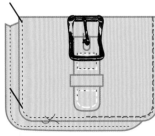

Flesh side

5 Attach parts to gusset.

Moisten D-ring stub.

Insert D-ring.

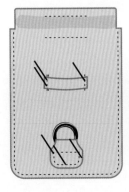

Moisten top edge of main body side gusset.
Glue belt loop and D-ring stub on gusset while aligning stitching holes.

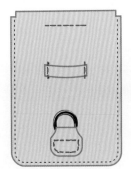

Fold down top edge of side gusset and glue down, while aligning stitching holes. Sew. Sew belt loop and D-ring stub on gusset.

1 Attach pocket on main body front.
Glue while aligning stitching holes.
Then, temporarily secure in place to prevent shifting.

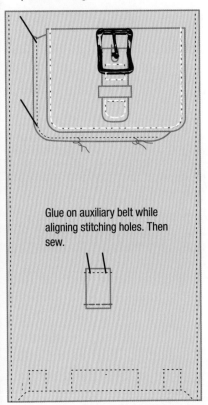

Glue on auxiliary belt while aligning stitching holes. Then sew.

2 Sew on pocket.

3 Glue flap on main body front while aligning stitching holes.

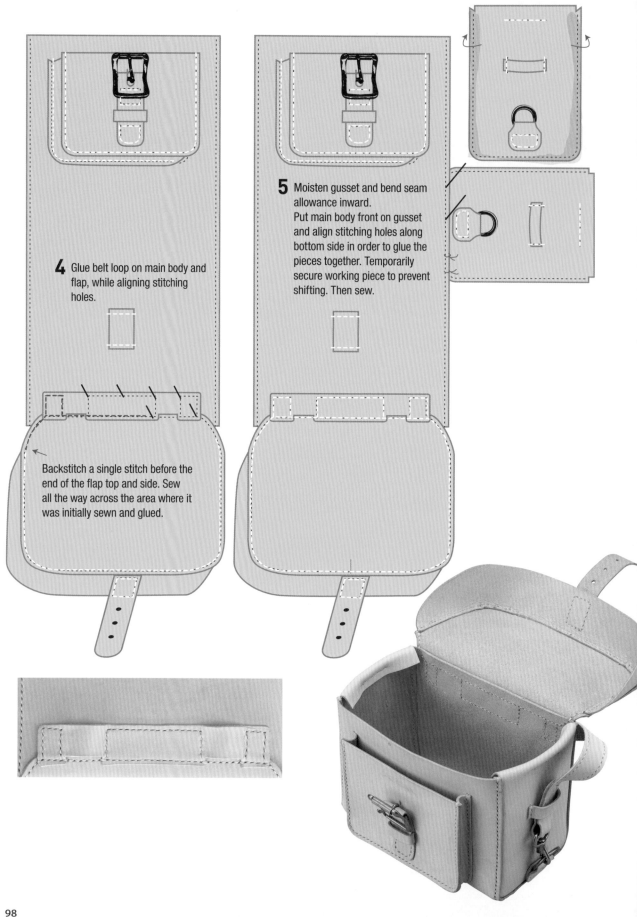

4 Glue belt loop on main body and flap, while aligning stitching holes.

Backstitch a single stitch before the end of the flap top and side. Sew all the way across the area where it was initially sewn and glued.

5 Moisten gusset and bend seam allowance inward.
Put main body front on gusset and align stitching holes along bottom side in order to glue the pieces together. Temporarily secure working piece to prevent shifting. Then sew.

Patterns

Flap position

Bicycle bag: belt position

Bicycle bag: belt loop
position for auxiliary belt

Main body front

Main body front

Pocket position

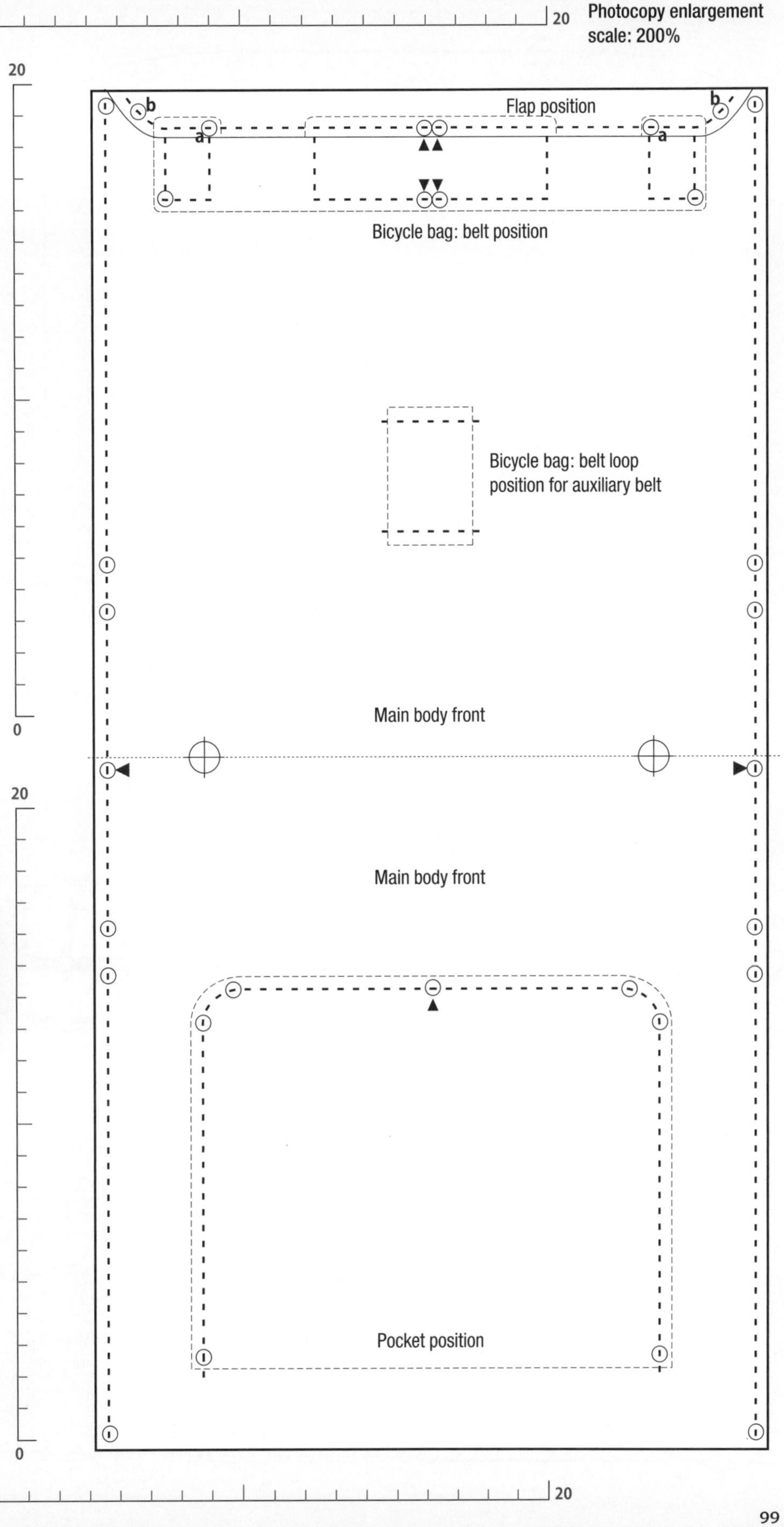

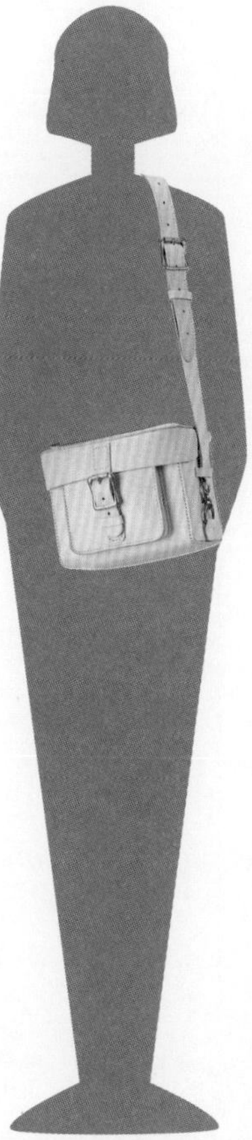

Patterns

Photocopy enlargement
scale: 200%

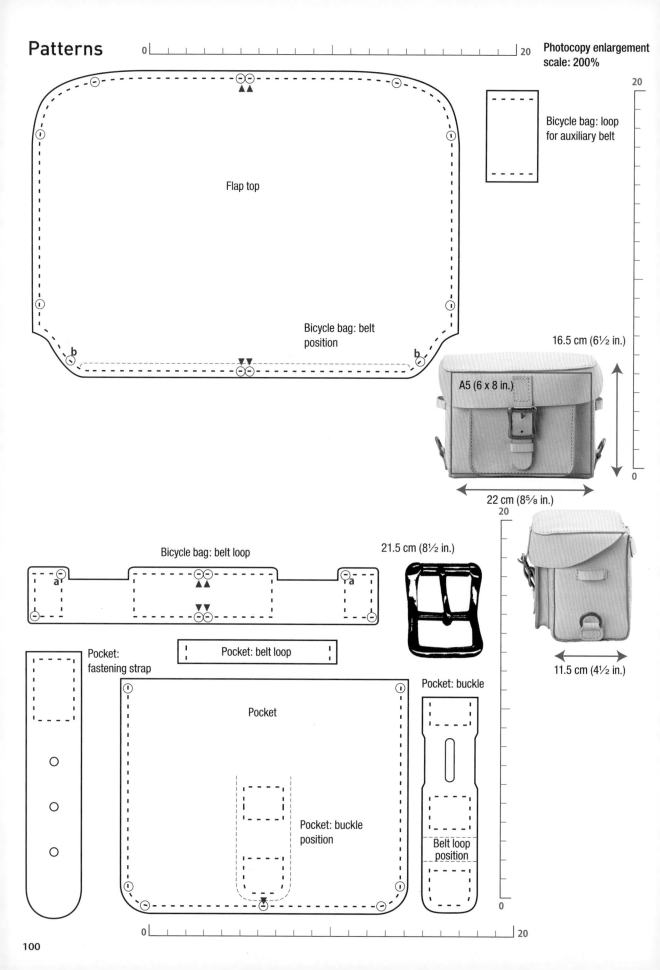

Flap top

Bicycle bag: belt
position

Bicycle bag: loop
for auxiliary belt

16.5 cm (6½ in.)

A5 (6 x 8 in.)

22 cm (8⅝ in.)

Bicycle bag: belt loop

21.5 cm (8½ in.)

11.5 cm (4½ in.)

Pocket:
fastening strap

Pocket: belt loop

Pocket

Pocket: buckle

Pocket: buckle
position

Belt loop
position

100

Patterns

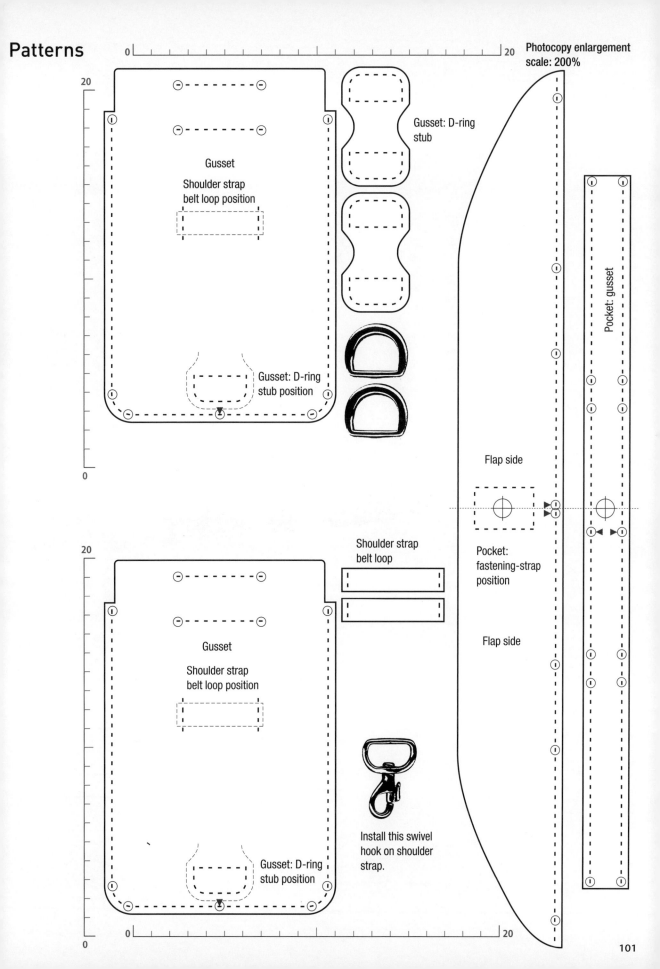

0   20

Photocopy enlargement scale: 200%

Gusset

Shoulder strap belt loop position

Gusset: D-ring stub position

Gusset: D-ring stub

Shoulder strap belt loop

Gusset

Shoulder strap belt loop position

Gusset: D-ring stub position

Install this swivel hook on shoulder strap.

Flap side

Pocket: fastening-strap position

Flap side

Pocket: gusset

Front

Side

Detail

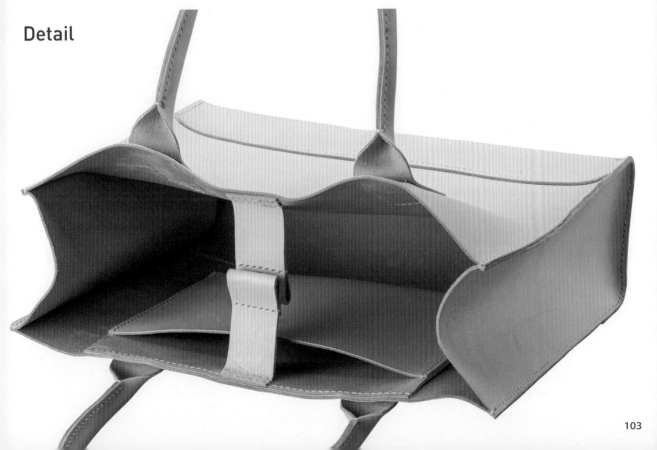

How To:

See "Installing Magnet Clasp," p. 48
See "Three-Dimensional Bonding," p. 52.

Punching Stitching Holes and Cutting Leather

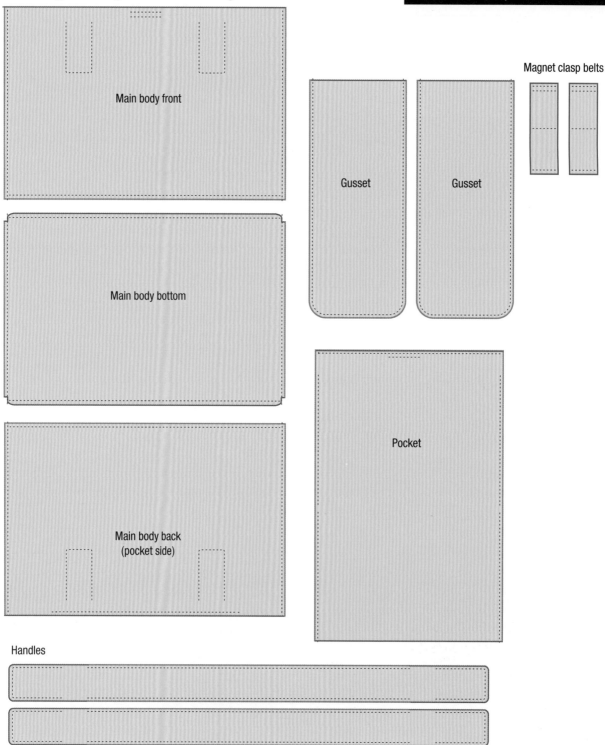

Main body front

Gusset

Gusset

Magnet clasp belts

Main body bottom

Pocket

Main body back
(pocket side)

Handles

- Apply burnishing agent to flesh side and
  edges marked with red lines.
- Transfer ○ marks from the pattern onto
  flesh side of leather.

Creating Parts and Attaching to the Main Body

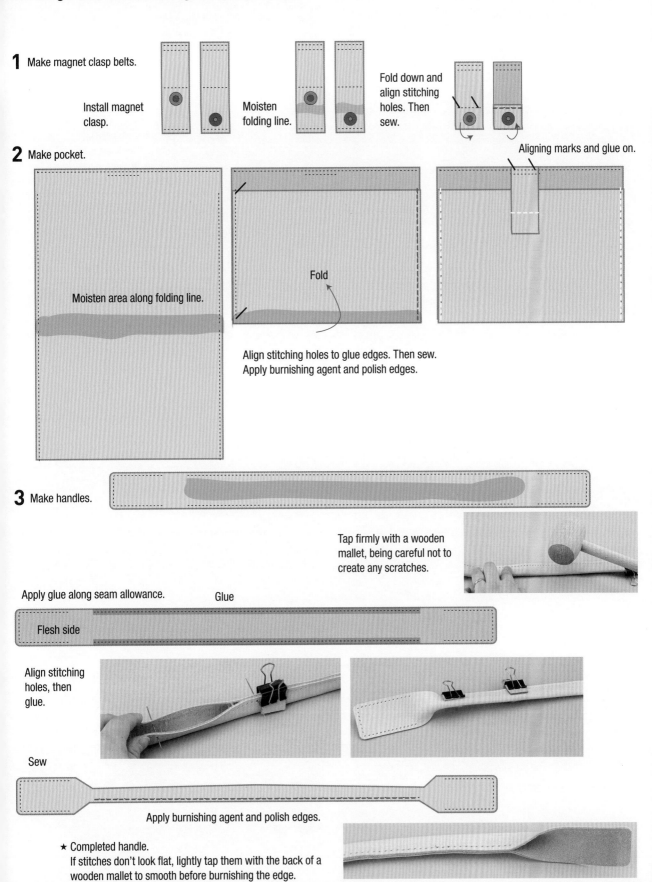

1 Make magnet clasp belts.

Install magnet clasp.

Moisten folding line.

Fold down and align stitching holes. Then sew.

Aligning marks and glue on.

2 Make pocket.

Moisten area along folding line.

Fold

Align stitching holes to glue edges. Then sew.
Apply burnishing agent and polish edges.

3 Make handles.

Tap firmly with a wooden mallet, being careful not to create any scratches.

Apply glue along seam allowance.   Glue

Flesh side

Align stitching holes, then glue.

Sew

Apply burnishing agent and polish edges.

★ Completed handle.
If stitches don't look flat, lightly tap them with the back of a wooden mallet to smooth before burnishing the edge.

Creating the Main Body

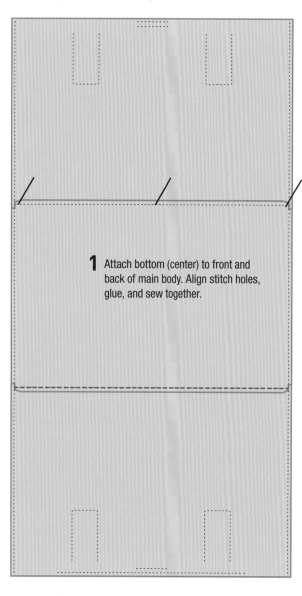

1 Attach bottom (center) to front and back of main body. Align stitch holes, glue, and sew together.

2 Moisten gusset and bend seam allowance outward.

Gusset

3 Glue gusset on working piece while aligning stitching holes. Then sew on gusset.

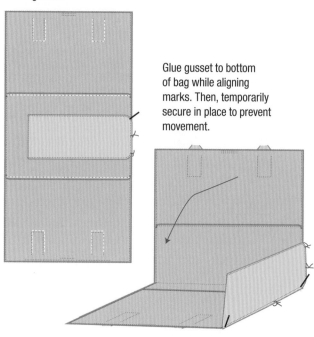

Glue gusset to bottom of bag while aligning marks. Then, temporarily secure in place to prevent movement.

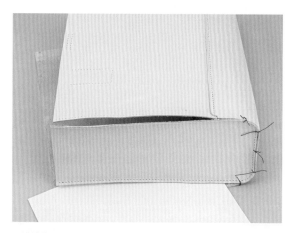

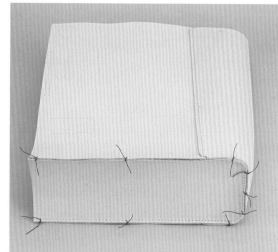

4 Attach handles to main body.
Align stitching holes, glue, then sew.

Stitching complete

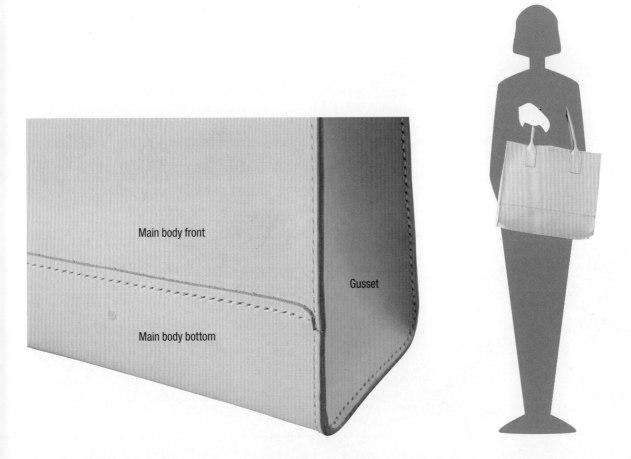

Main body front

Gusset

Main body bottom

5 Align stitching holes, glue, and sew magnetic belt to front of main body.

Sew

6 Align stitching holes and glue. Then, sew magnetic belt and pocket together onto back of main body all at once.

Sew while avoiding handles.

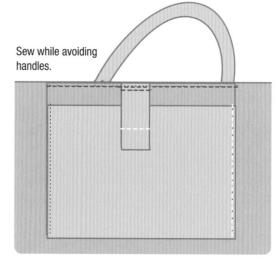

Patterns

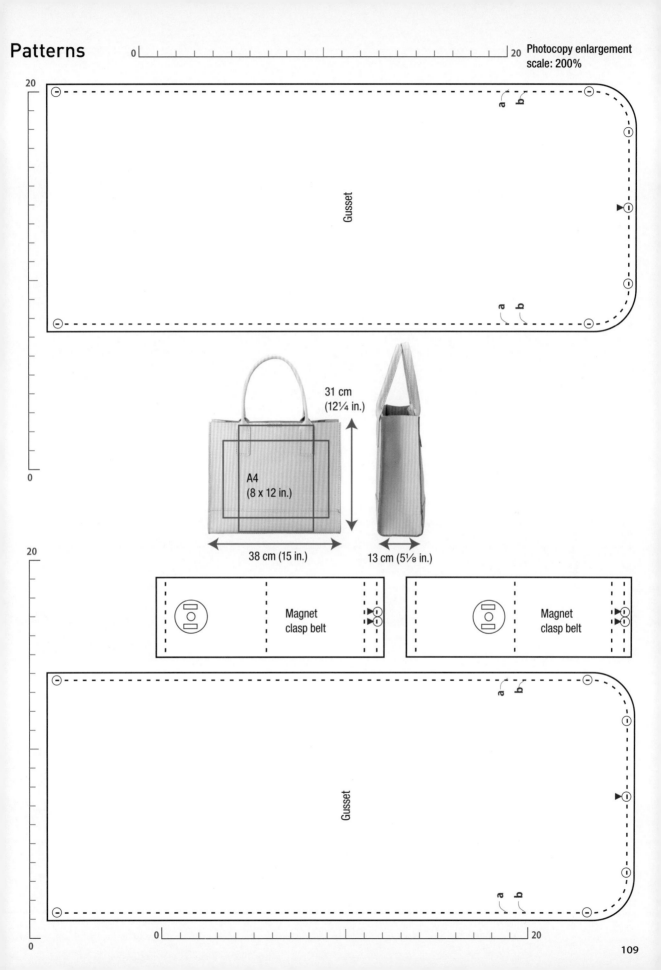

Gusset

31 cm (12¼ in.)

A4 (8 x 12 in.)

38 cm (15 in.)

13 cm (5⅛ in.)

Magnet clasp belt

Magnet clasp belt

Gusset

Patterns

Photocopy enlargement
scale: 200%

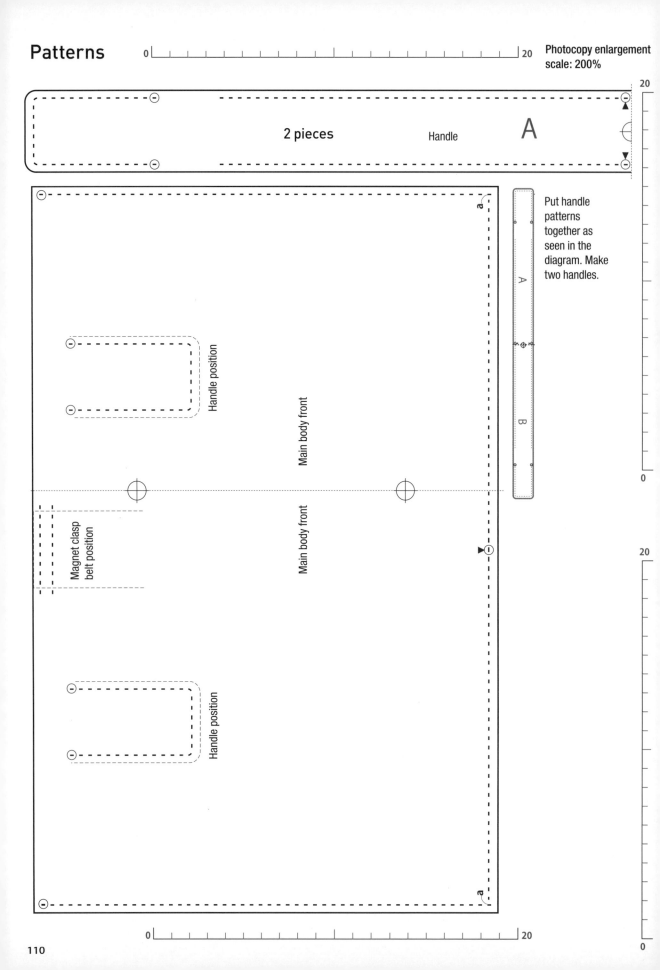

2 pieces   Handle   A

Put handle
patterns
together as
seen in the
diagram. Make
two handles.

A

B

Handle position

Main body front

Main body front

Magnet clasp
belt position

Handle position

0 |_____| 20

Patterns

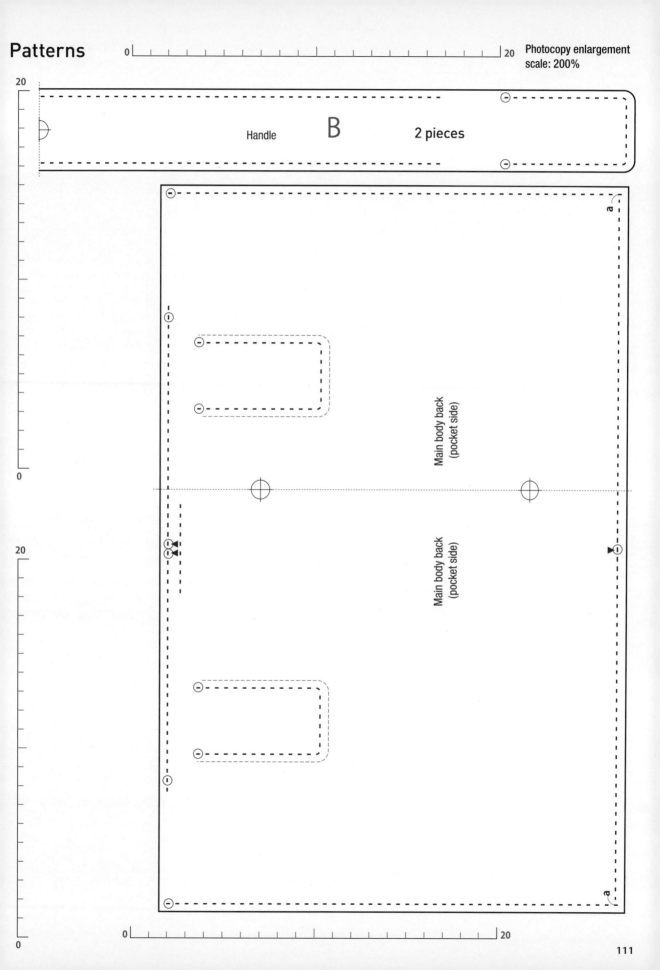

Handle B 2 pieces

Main body back (pocket side)

Main body back (pocket side)

111

Patterns

Photocopy enlargement
scale: 200%

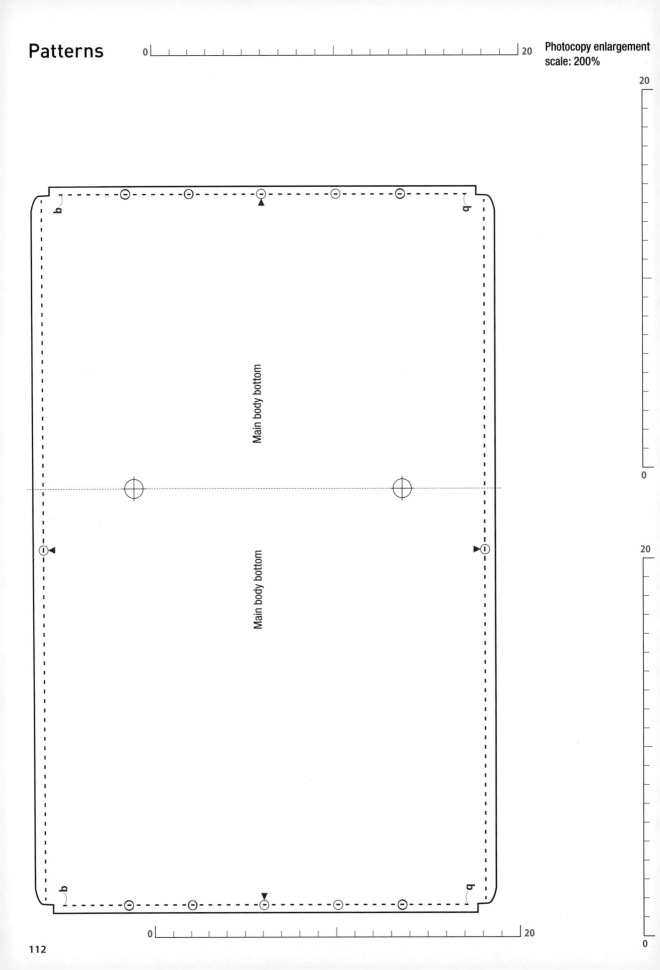

Main body bottom

Main body bottom

Patterns

Photocopy enlargement
scale: 200%

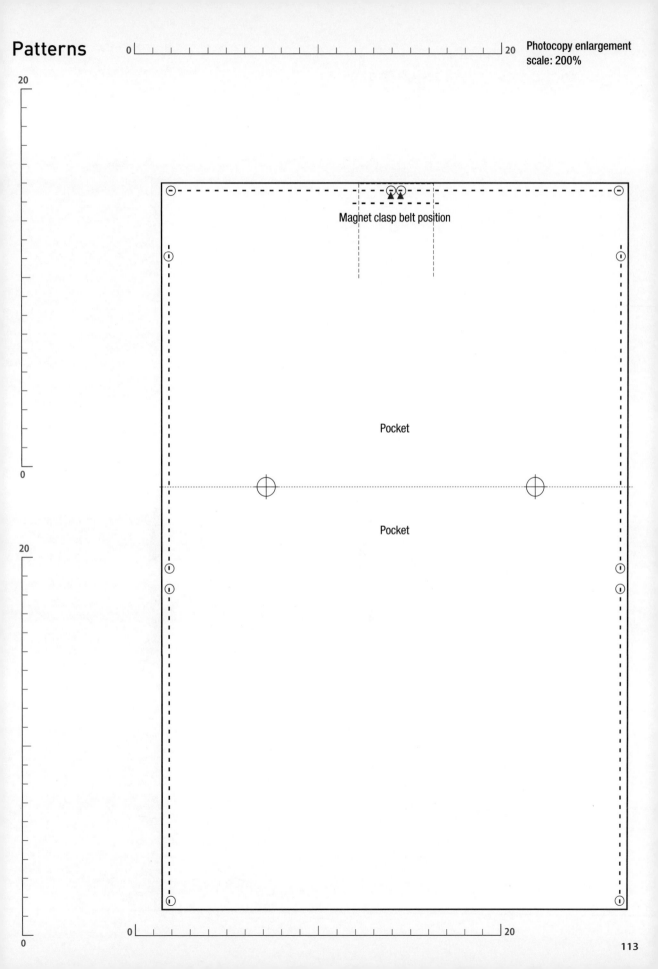

Magnet clasp belt position

Pocket

Pocket

Front

Side

Detail

How To:

Punching Out Stitching Holes and Cutting Leather

See "How to Make Shoulder Strap and Pattern," p. 40–47.
  Stitched along edges.
See "Making a Folded Handle," p. 44.
See "Installing Sam Browne Stud," p. 48
See "Three-Dimensional Bonding," p. 52.

Shoulder strap

Main body front

Main body back

Main body side

Pocket

Handle

Handle

Main body bottom

D-ring stub

Belt loop

- Apply burnishing agent to flesh side and the edges marked with red lines.
- Transfer ○ from pattern onto flesh side of leather.

Fastening strap

Main body side

Creating Parts and Attaching to Main Body

1 Make handles.

Stitch both ends until marked position.

Moisten handle and fold in half lengthwise.
Align stitching holes up to marked position.

Sew

★ If you want to stitch all the way around the handle, just continue sewing to the end. Apply burnishing agent and polish edges.

2 Attach belt loop for strap to the pocket. Align stitching holes and sew. Attach Sam Browne stud.

3 Attach strap and pocket to main body front. Align stitching holes, and sew.

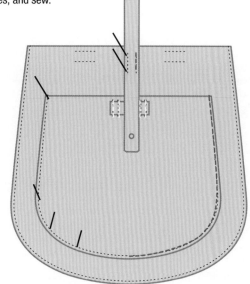

4 Attach handles to back side of main body. Align stitching holes, and sew.

Main body front

Flesh side

5 Attach belt loop for fastening strap to main body back. Align stitching holes and sew. Attach handle to back side of main body in the same way as the main body front. Align stitching holes and sew.

Install Sam Browne stud

6 Moisten D-ring stub and fold in half.

Pass D-ring stub through D-ring. Sandwich top of gusset with D-ring stub. Align stitching holes with top edge of gusset, glue, and sew.

Creating Main Body

1 Glue and sew main body side to bottom. Align stitching holes.

2 Moisten and bend seam allowance of main body back.

3 Glue main body side to back. Align stitching holes, and temporarily secure working piece to prevent shifting.

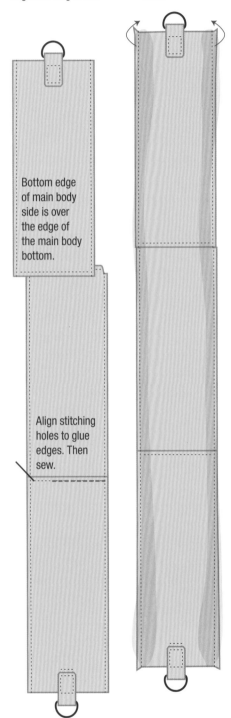

Bottom edge of main body side is over the edge of the main body bottom.

Align stitching holes to glue edges. Then sew.

Align stitching holes. Then glue.

Temporarily secure in place to prevent shifting.

4 Glue main body side to the back. Align stitching holes and temporarily secure working piece to prevent shifting.

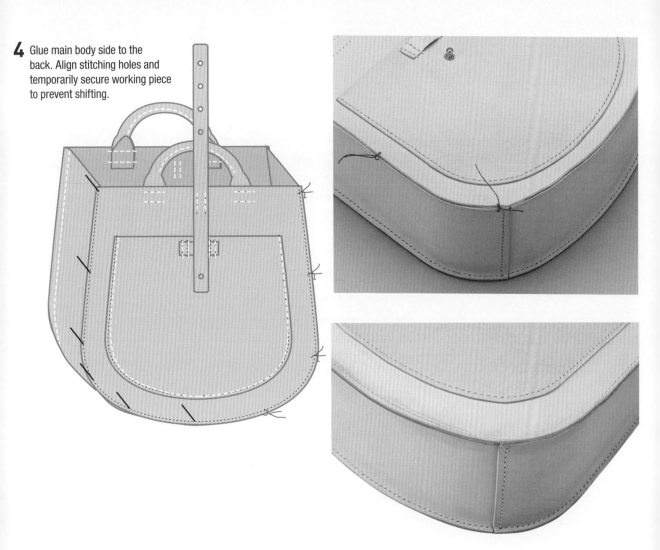

Two-Ply Shoulder Strap

One-ply where leather is folded

Align with one edge.

Turn inside out and punch stitching holes all the way through to the backside.

Three-ply here

Align stitching holes. Then glue.

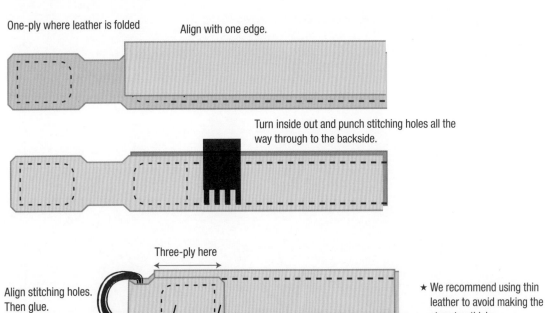

★ We recommend using thin leather to avoid making the strap too thick.

Patterns

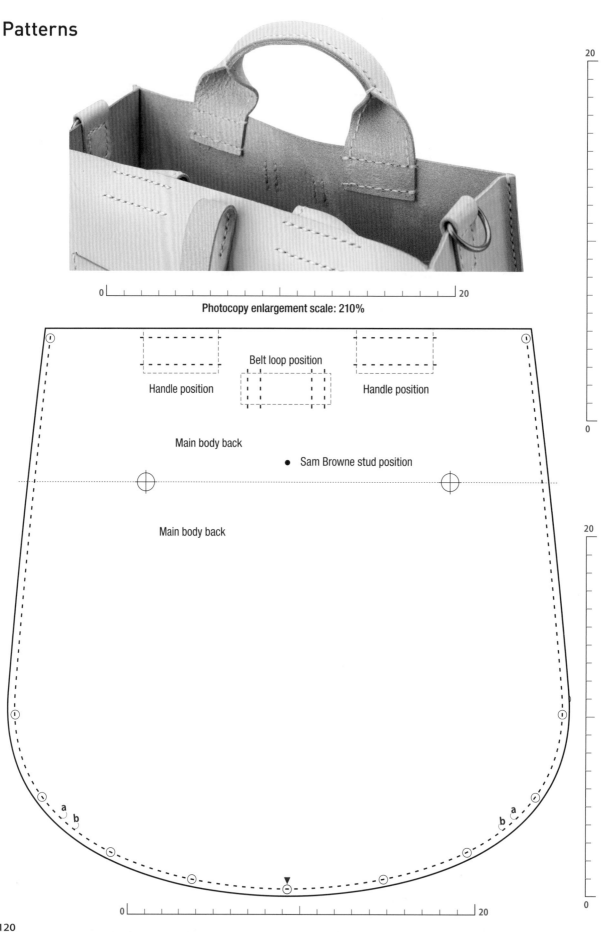

Photocopy enlargement scale: 210%

Handle position

Belt loop position

Handle position

Main body back

● Sam Browne stud position

Main body back

a
b

b
a

Patterns

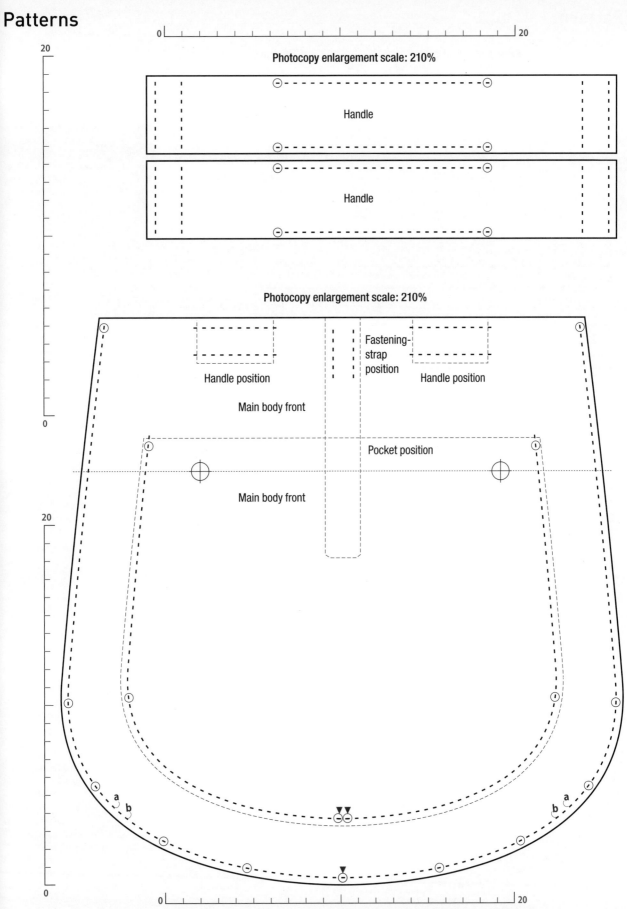

Photocopy enlargement scale: 210%

Handle

Handle

Photocopy enlargement scale: 210%

Handle position

Fastening-strap position

Handle position

Main body front

Pocket position

Main body front

a b

b a

Patterns

Photocopy enlargement
scale: 200%

20

Shoulder strap: cut leather 30 mm (1¼ in.) wide and 720 mm (28⅜ in.) long.
Add pattern of swivel hook belt to shoulder strap. Then punch stitching holes and sew.

Shoulder strap   Shoulder strap

A   B

As for the strap, put patterns together as
shown in the diagram.

A

Fastening strap

B

Fastening strap

Belt loop   Belt loop

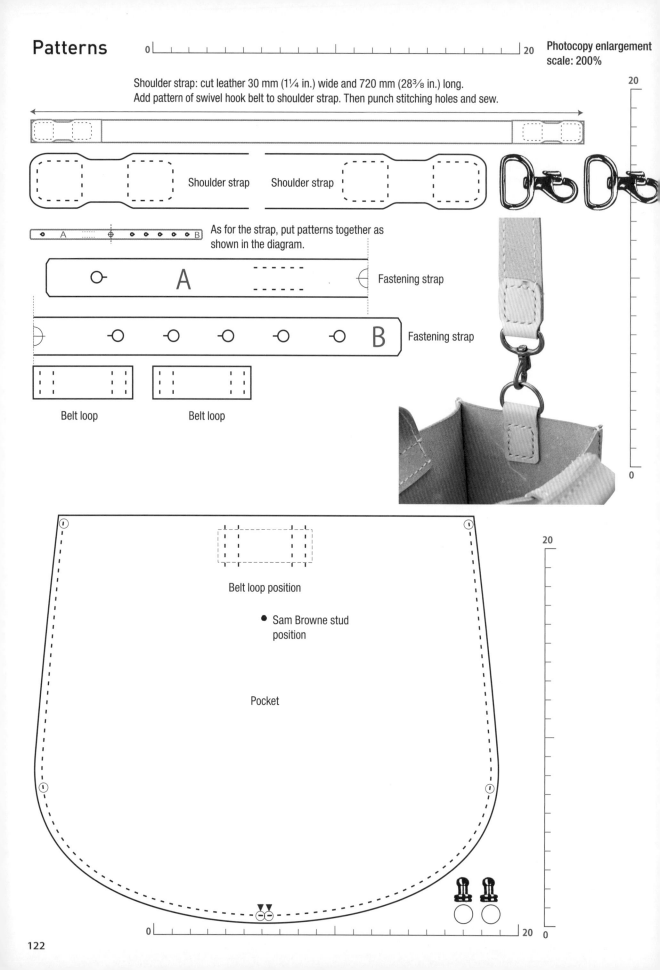

20

0

Belt loop position

• Sam Browne stud
position

Pocket

20

0   20   0

Patterns

Photocopy enlargement
scale: 200%

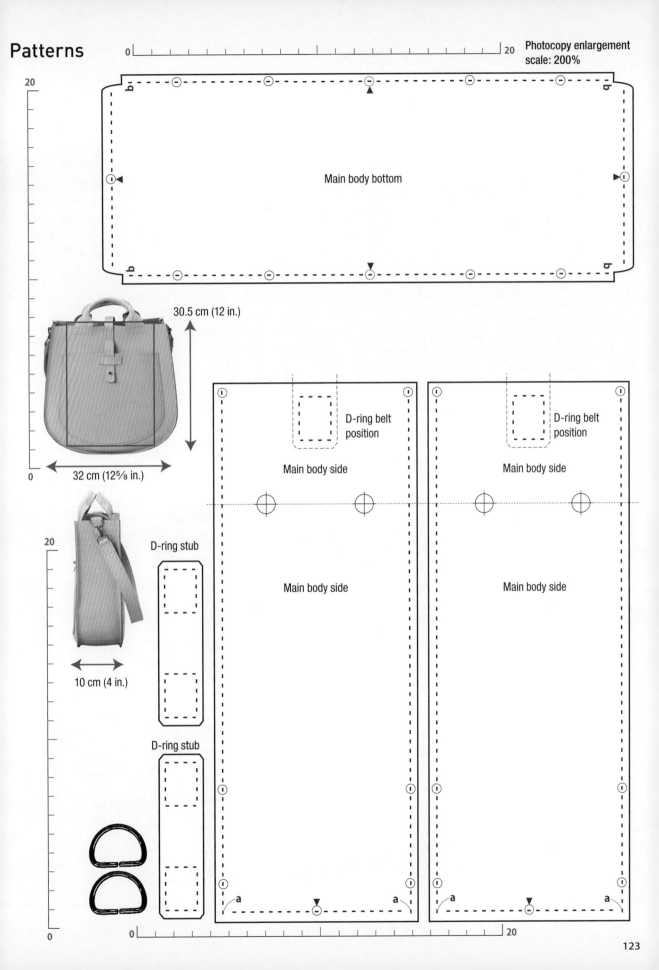

Main body bottom

30.5 cm (12 in.)

32 cm (12⅝ in.)

10 cm (4 in.)

D-ring stub

D-ring stub

D-ring belt
position

Main body side

Main body side

D-ring belt
position

Main body side

Main body side

Front

Side

Detail

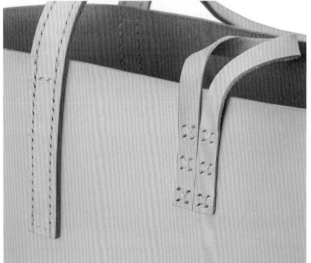

How To:

See "Creating a Simple Handle," p. 40–45.
Two-ply and stitched along edges.
See "Stitching Turned Edges," p. 53.

Punching Stitching Holes and Cutting Leather

- Apply burnishing agent to flesh side and edges marked with red lines.
- Transfer ○ marks on pattern to flesh side of leather.

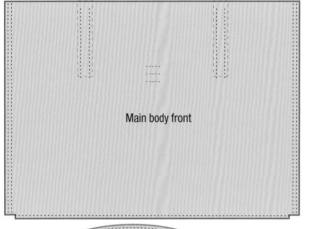

Main body front

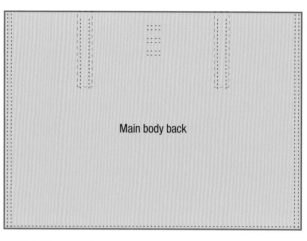

Main body back

Hook belt
Cord
Leather knob

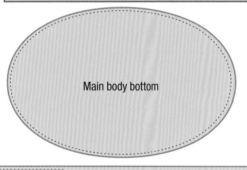

Main body bottom

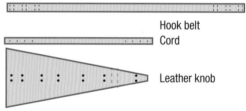

Make each handle two-ply.

Creating Parts and Attaching to Main Body

1 Punch small holes, about 3 mm (⅛ in.) diameter, on leather knob.

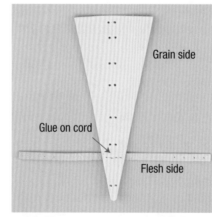

Grain side

Glue on cord

Flesh side

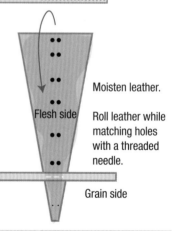

Moisten leather.

Roll leather while matching holes with a threaded needle.

Flesh side

Grain side

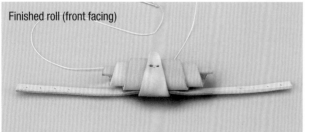

Finished roll (front facing)

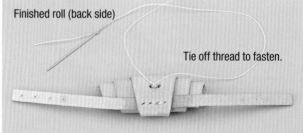

Finished roll (back side)

Tie off thread to fasten.

2 Attach handle and leather fastener strings to front of main body. Align with seam holes, and adhere.

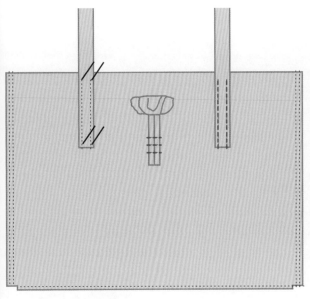

Glue handles and hook belt to main body back while aligning stitching holes.

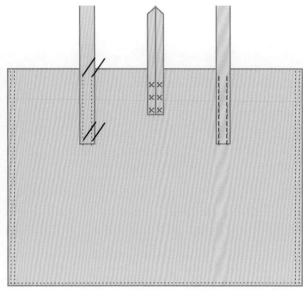

Creating Main Body

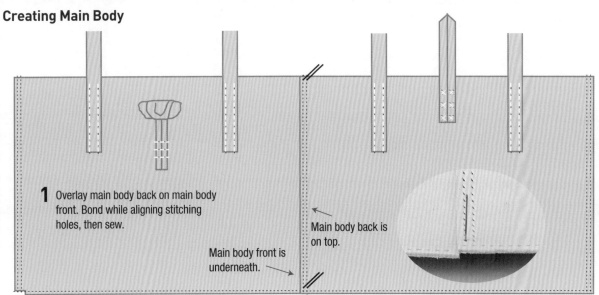

1 Overlay main body back on main body front. Bond while aligning stitching holes, then sew.

Main body back is on top.

Main body front is underneath.

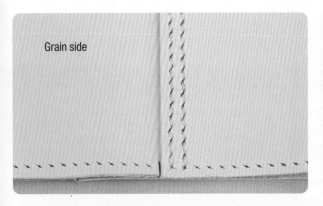

Grain side

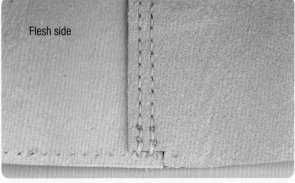

Flesh side

2 Create a tube shape by gluing sides together while aligning stitching holes.

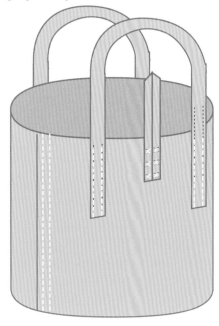

Sew

Stitching is complete.

3 Moisten and bend bottom seam allowance inward.

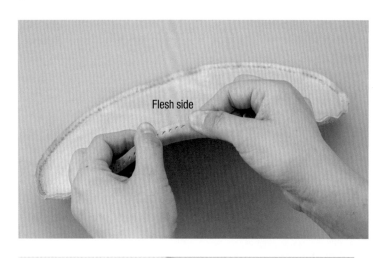

Flesh side

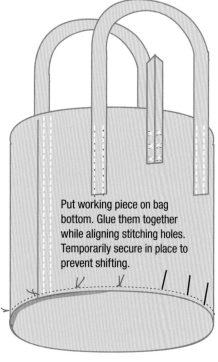

Put working piece on bag bottom. Glue them together while aligning stitching holes. Temporarily secure in place to prevent shifting.

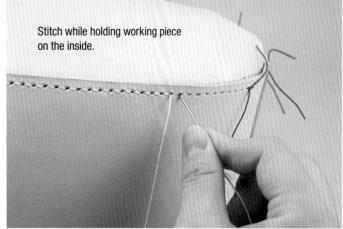

Stitch while holding working piece on the inside.

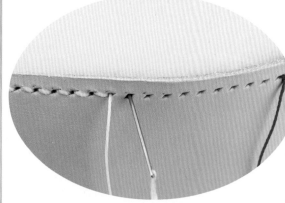

Patterns

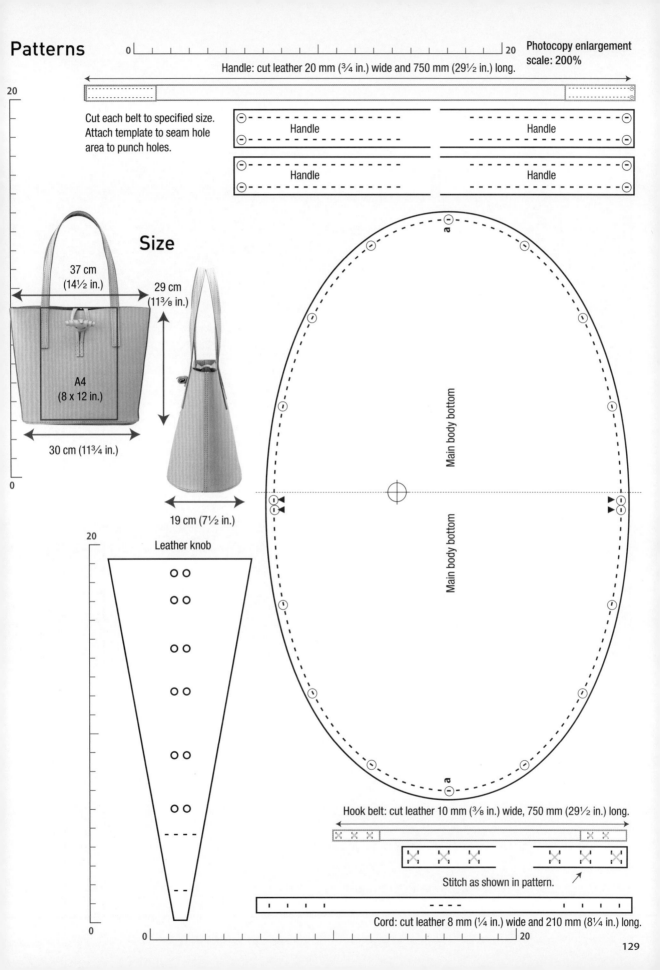

0 ————————————————— 20

Photocopy enlargement
scale: 200%

Handle: cut leather 20 mm (¾ in.) wide and 750 mm (29½ in.) long.

Handle

Handle

Handle

Handle

Cut each belt to specified size.
Attach template to seam hole
area to punch holes.

Size

37 cm
(14½ in.)

29 cm
(11³⁄₈ in.)

A4
(8 x 12 in.)

30 cm (11¾ in.)

19 cm (7½ in.)

Main body bottom

Main body bottom

a

a

Leather knob

Hook belt: cut leather 10 mm (³⁄₈ in.) wide, 750 mm (29½ in.) long.

Stitch as shown in pattern.

Cord: cut leather 8 mm (¼ in.) wide and 210 mm (8¼ in.) long.

0 ————————————————— 20

Patterns

Photocopy enlargement scale: 200%

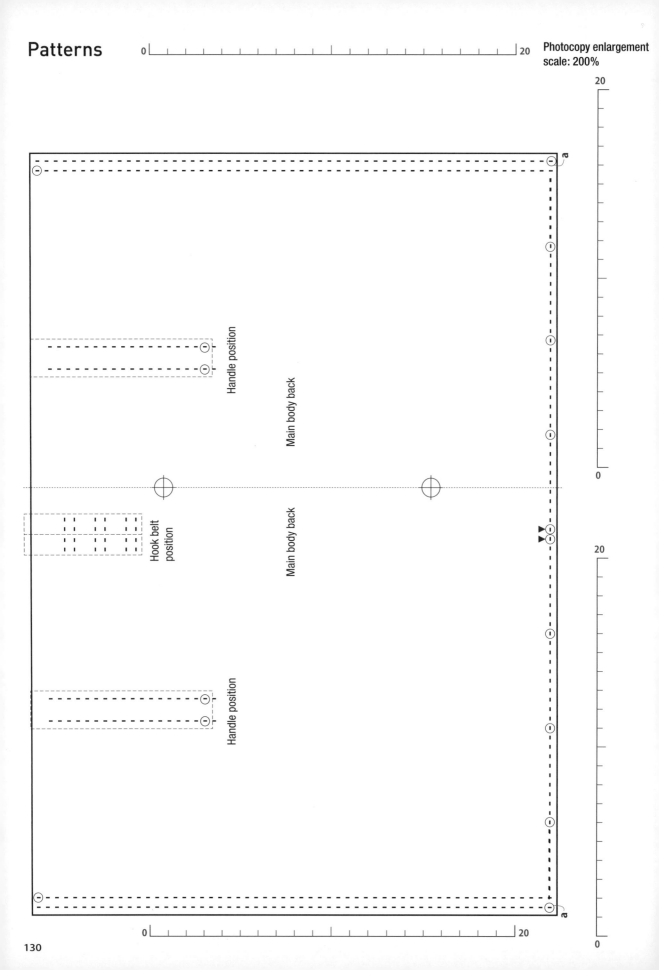

Handle position

Main body back

Main body back

Hook belt position

Handle position

130

Patterns

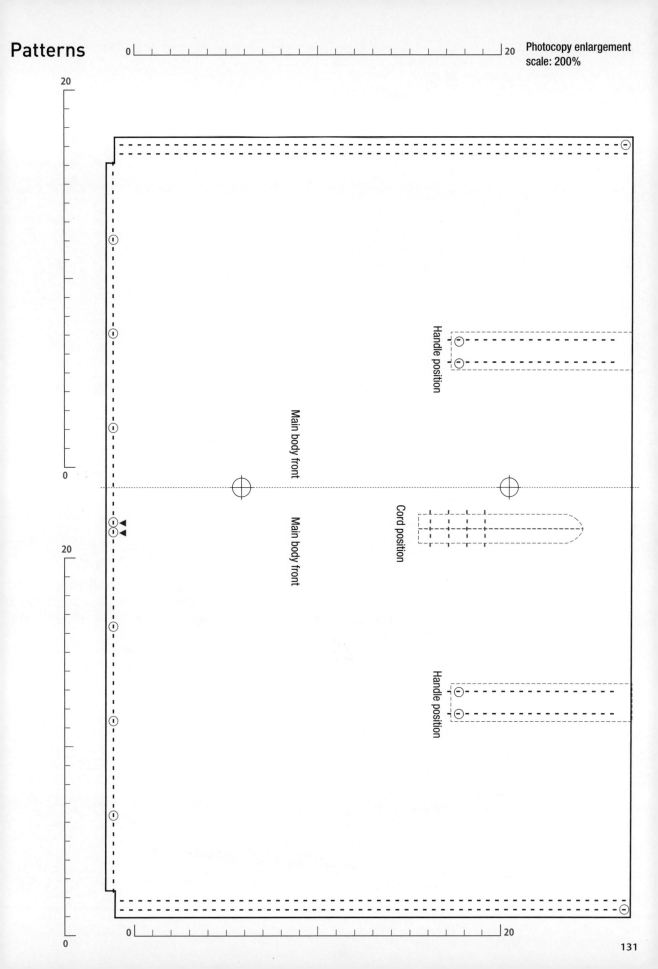

Main body front

Main body front

Handle position

Handle position

Cord position

Tanned Leather Bag No. 10
Messenger Bag

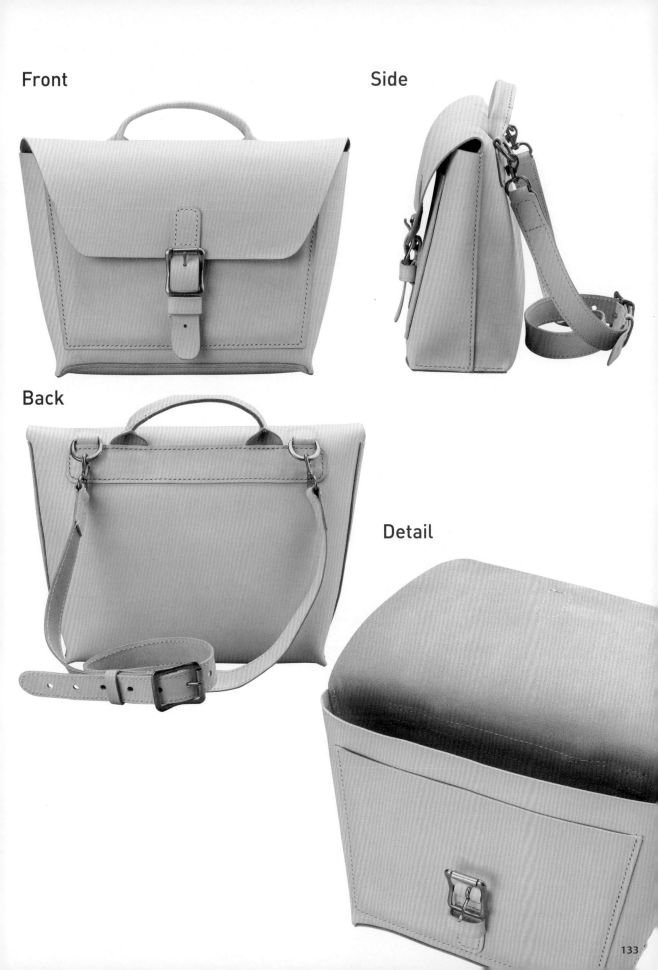

Front

Side

Back

Detail

133

How To:

Punching Stitching Holes and Cutting Leather

- Apply burnishing agent to flesh side and the edges marked with red lines.
- Transfer ○ marks on pattern to flesh side of leather.

See "How to Make Shoulder Strap and Pattern," p. 40–47.
 Stitch along the edges.
See "Making a Folded Handle," p. 44.
See "Attaching Buckle," p. 46–47.
See "Stitching Turned Edges," p. 53.
See "Stitching Three Pieces of Leather, or More, at Once," p. 58.

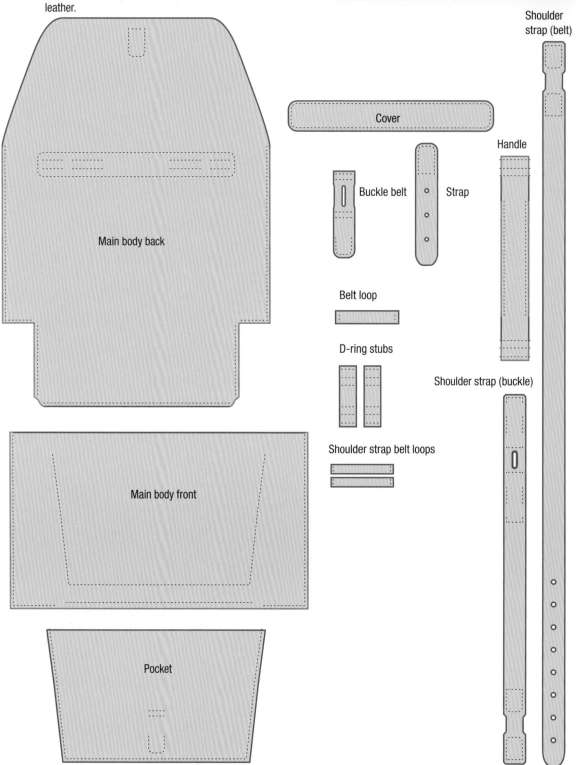

Shoulder strap (belt)

Cover

Handle

Buckle belt

Strap

Main body back

Belt loop

D-ring stubs

Shoulder strap (buckle)

Shoulder strap belt loops

Main body front

Pocket

Creating Parts and Attaching to Main Body

1 Moisten handle.

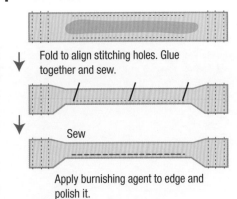

Fold to align stitching holes. Glue together and sew.

Sew

Apply burnishing agent to edge and polish it.

2 Moisten D-ring stub.

Insert D-ring stub through D-ring. Align stitching holes and glue belt ends together.

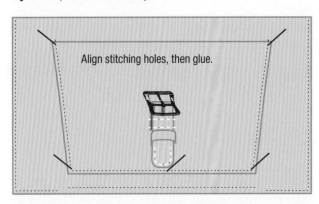

3 Making belt buckle to attach to pocket

Moisten belt loop.

Add buckle to belt.

Fold to make a circle.

Sew

Thread belt loop.

Moisten and fold. Align stitching holes and then glue.

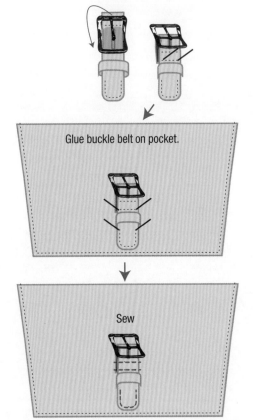

Glue buckle belt on pocket.

Sew

4 Attach pocket on main body.

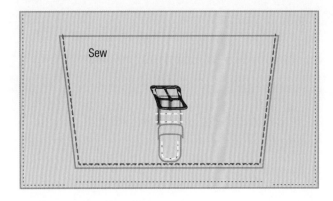

Align stitching holes, then glue.

Sew

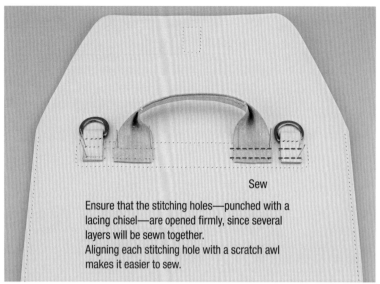

Sew

Ensure that the stitching holes—punched with a lacing chisel—are opened firmly, since several layers will be sewn together.
Aligning each stitching hole with a scratch awl makes it easier to sew.

5 Glue D-ring stub and handle to main body back. Align stitching holes.

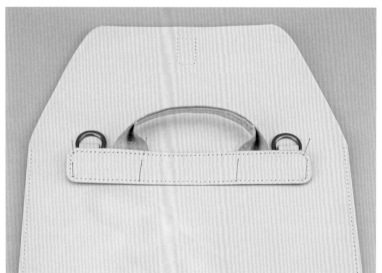

6 Glue cover to main body back. Align stitching holes.

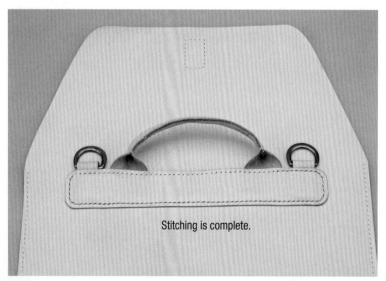

Stitching is complete.

7 Sew on cover.

Creating Main Body

1 Glue strap to main body back while aligning stitching holes.

Sew

2 Glue main body front on main body back. Align stitching holes and sew.

The main body back is on top.

The main body front is underneath.

3 Glue main body front gusset to main body back. Align stitching holes, and sew.

The main body back is underneath.

The main body front is on top.

4 Layer gussets of main body front and back together. Glue while aligning stitching holes and sew.

Main body front

Main body back

Main body back (bottom)

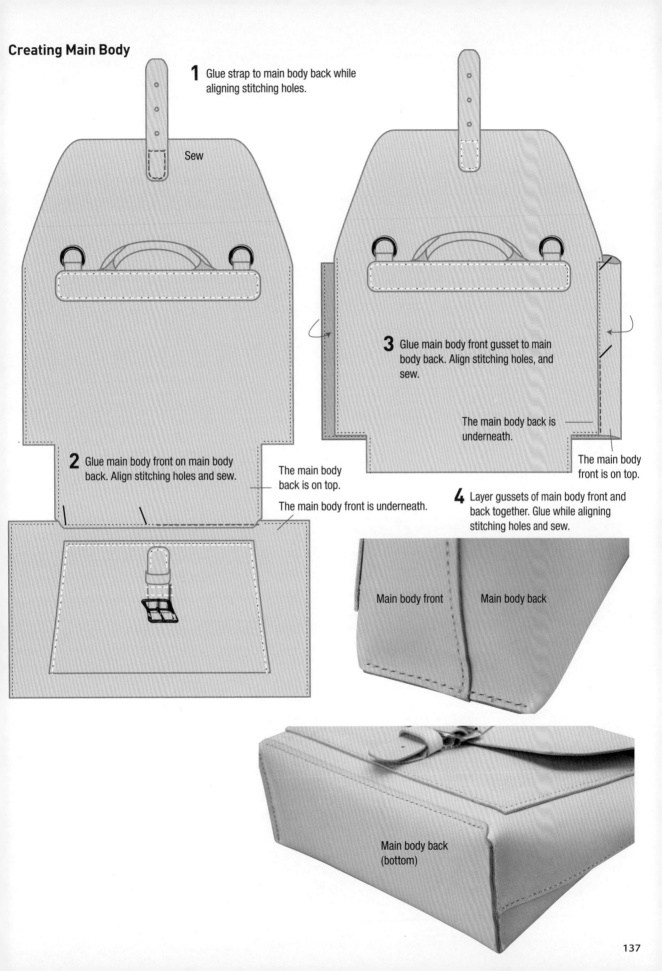

Patterns

Photocopy enlargement
scale: 200%

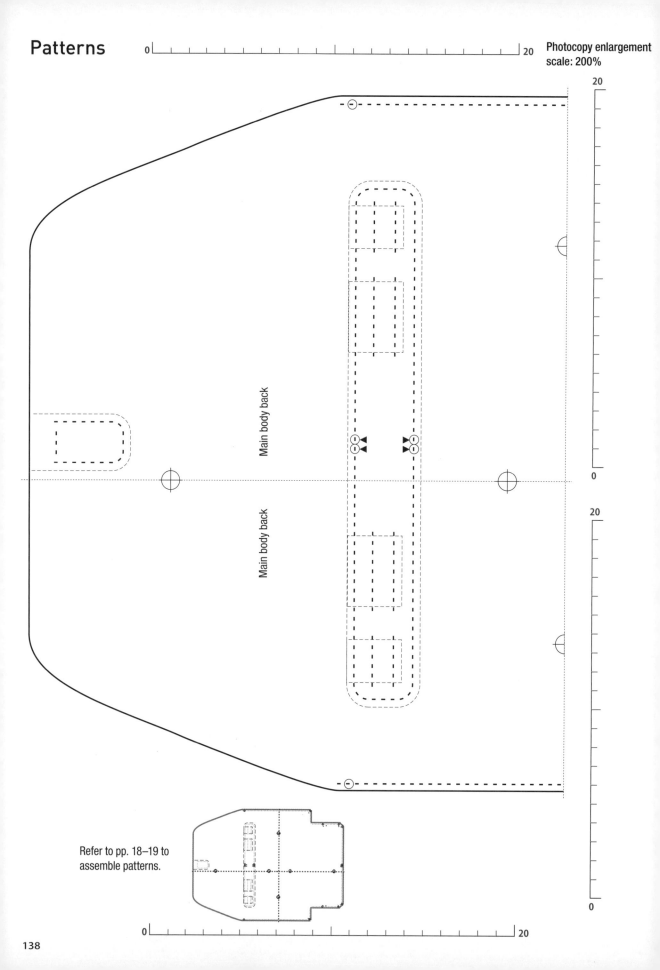

Main body back

Main body back

20

0

20

0

Refer to pp. 18–19 to
assemble patterns.

0 |⎵⎵⎵⎵⎵⎵⎵⎵⎵⎵⎵⎵⎵⎵⎵| 20

138

Patterns

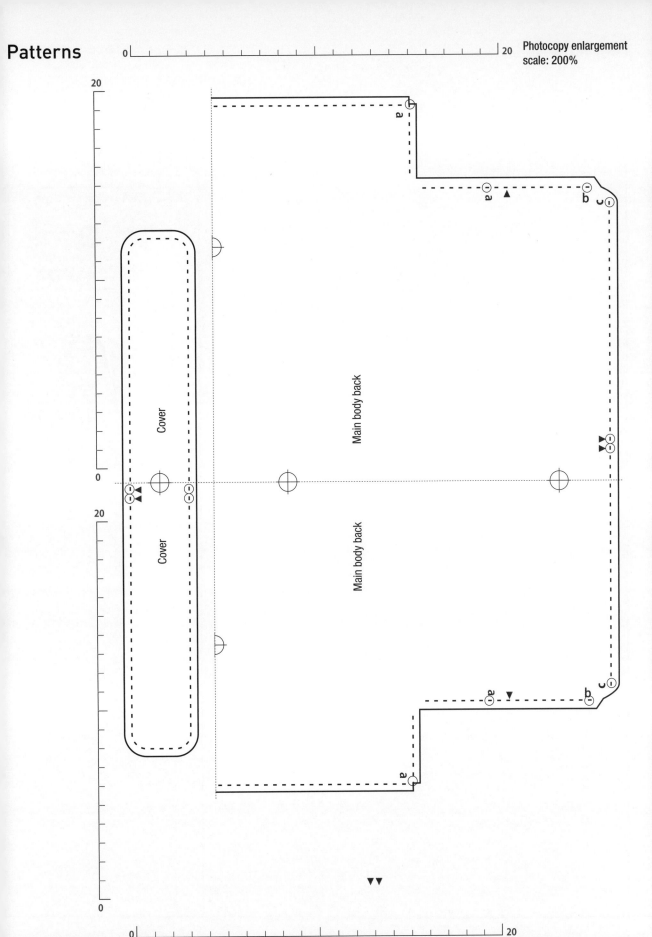

Patterns

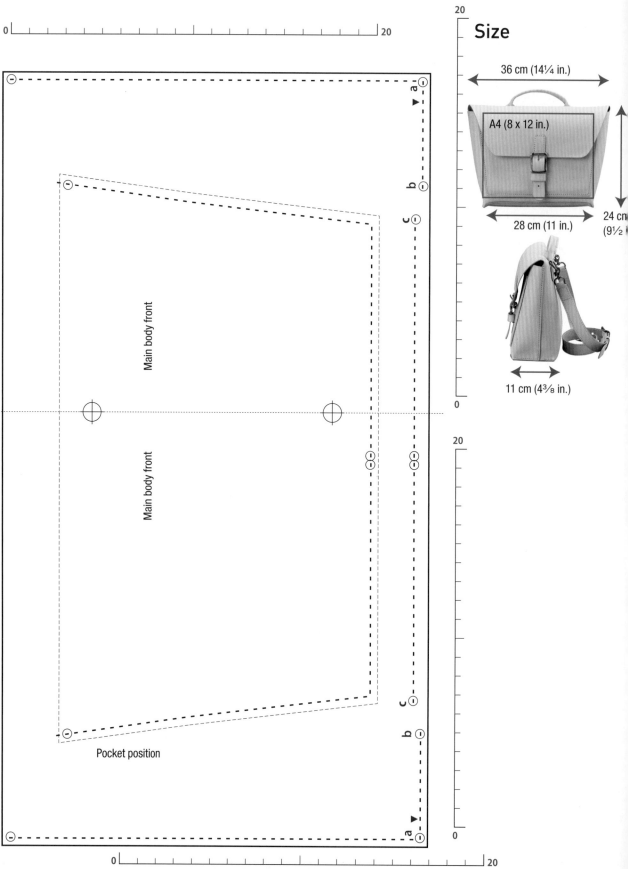

0 — 20

20

Size

36 cm (14¼ in.)

A4 (8 x 12 in.)

28 cm (11 in.)

24 cm
(9½

11 cm (4⅜ in.)

Main body front

Main body front

Pocket position

a

b

c

a

b

c

0

20

Patterns

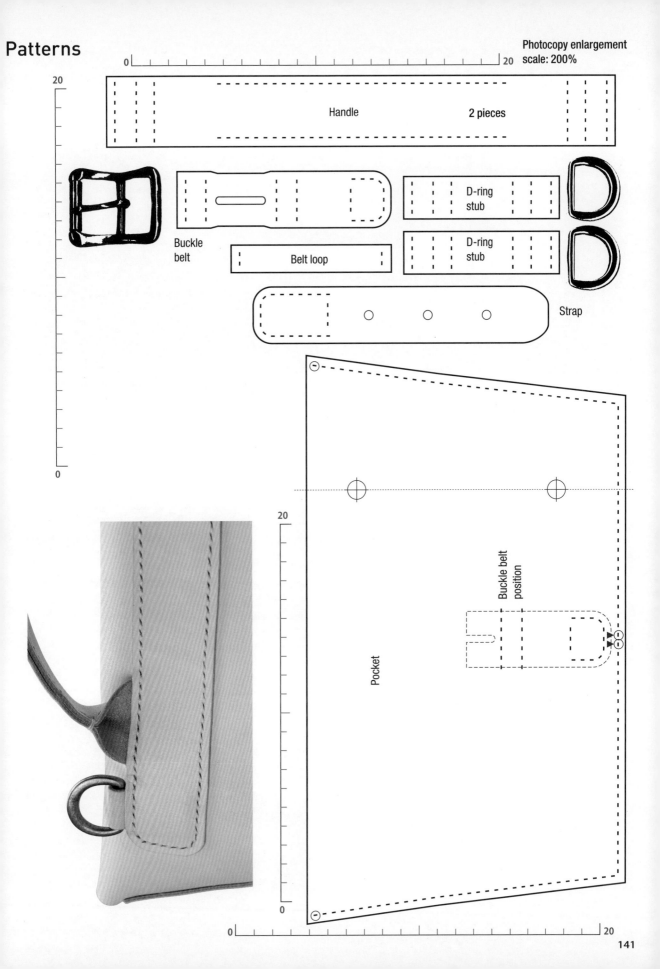

0   20

20

0

Handle   2 pieces

Buckle belt

D-ring stub

D-ring stub

Belt loop

Strap

Pocket

Buckle belt position

20

0

0   20

Tanned Leather Bag No. 11
Circle-Shaped Handbag

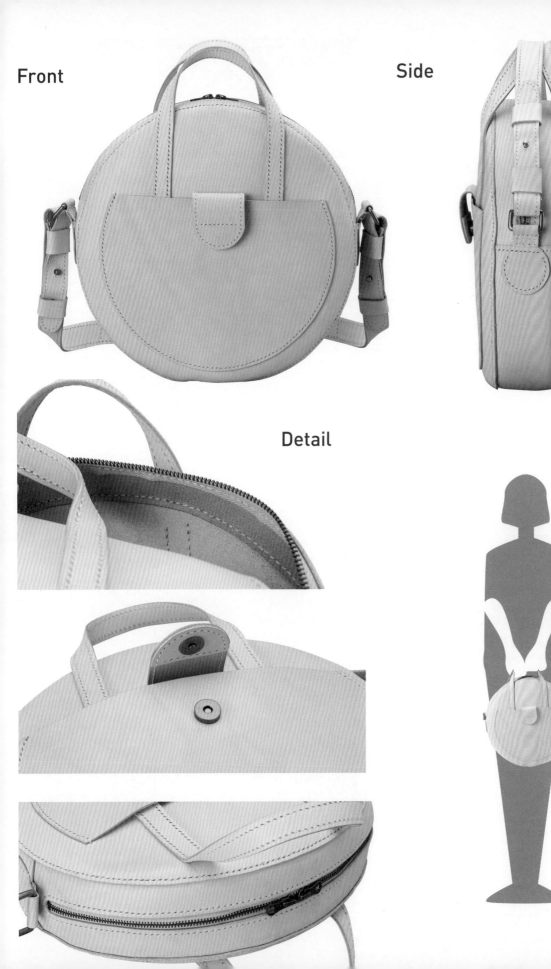

Front

Side

Detail

143

How To:

Punching Stitching Holes and Cutting Leather

- Apply burnishing agent to flesh side and to edges marked with red lines.
- Transfer ○ marks on the pattern to flesh side of leather.

See "How to Make Shoulder Strap and Pattern," p. 40–47.
  Stitch as specified in diagram.
See "Creating a Simple Handle," p. 40–43
  Two-ply and stitched along edges.
See "Installing Sam Browne Stud," p. 48
See "Installing a Zipper," p. 50–51
See "Stitching Turned Edges," p. 53.

Shoulder strap center

Main body front

Main body Back

Pocket

Main body side (upper)

Main body side (bottom)

Square D-ring stubs

Belt loops

Shoulder straps left, right

Magnet clasp belt

Handles

Cover

Creating Parts and Attaching to Main Body

1 Install magnet clasp (base) to pocket.

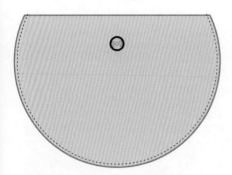

2 Install magnet clasp (stud) to belt.

3 Glue cover to magnetic belt. Align stitching holes, and sew.

4 Glue magnet clasp belt and then the pocket—in that order—to the main body front. Align stitching holes and sew.

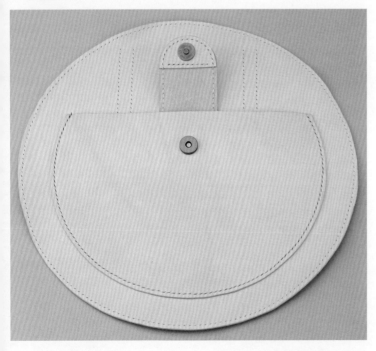

5 Install zipper to main body side (upper).

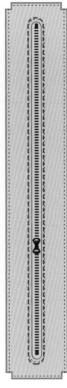

6 Attach square D-ring to main body side (bottom).

Moisten square D-ring stub.

Thread square D-ring through square D-ring stub. Align stitching holes, glue, and sew.

Do not sew here.

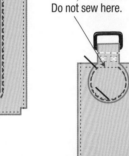

Align stitching holes on main body side (bottom), adhere, and sew.

Creating Main Body

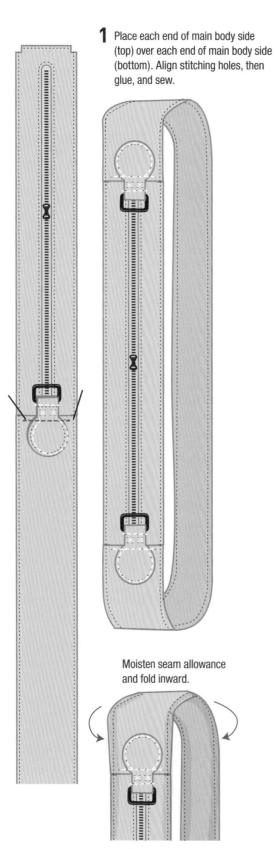

1 Place each end of main body side (top) over each end of main body side (bottom). Align stitching holes, then glue, and sew.

Moisten seam allowance and fold inward.

2 Overlay main body back onto main body side. Align stitching holes, then glue, and temporarily secure to prevent misalignment. Sew.

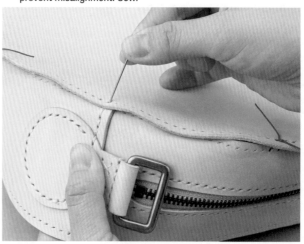

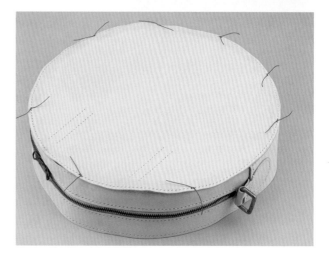

3 Overlay main body front onto main body side. Align stitching holes, glue, and temporarily secure to prevent misalignment. Sew.

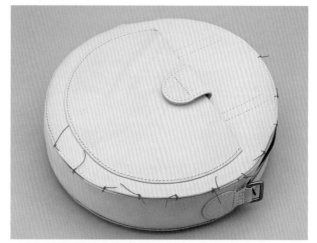

4 Unzip zipper and glue handle to main body. Align stitching holes, then sew.

5
Join both Bs to center of shoulder strap A. Align stitching holes, then sew.

6
Sandwich left and right shoulder straps —with belt loop—between shoulder strap center. Align stitching holes and then sew.

C

Shoulder straps left, right

Flesh side

Belt loop position

Sam Browne stud

Belt loop position

Shoulder strap center

B

Shoulder strap center

A

Shoulder strap center

B

Belt loop position

Sam Browne stud

Belt loop position

Fold belt loop, then sew.

Shoulder strap center

Shoulder straps left, right

Shoulder strap center

Flesh side

Shoulder straps left, right

C

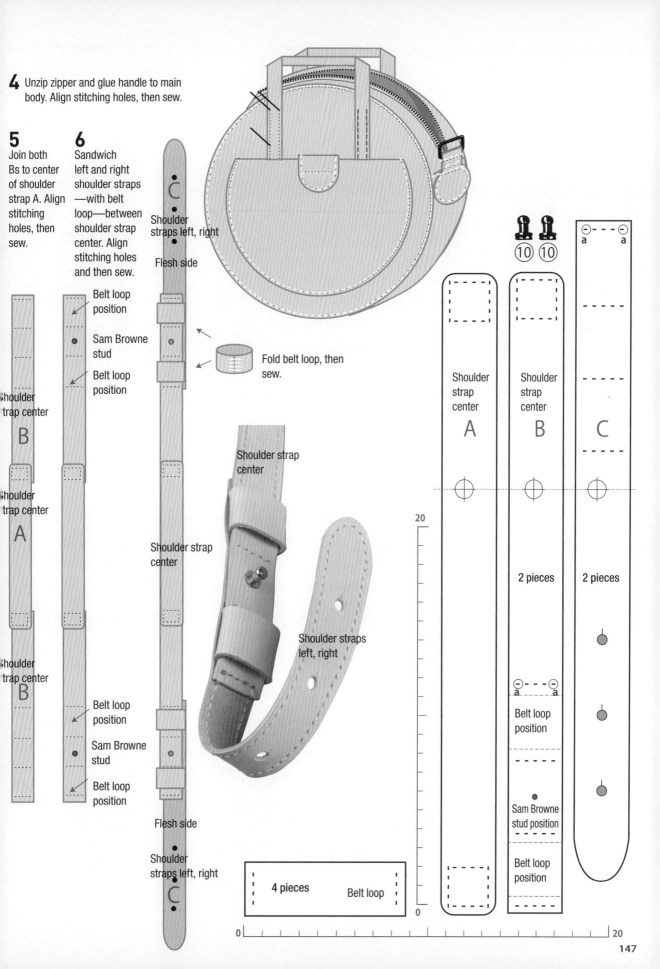

4 pieces   Belt loop

Shoulder strap center

A

Shoulder strap center

B

C

a   a

2 pieces

2 pieces

a   a

Belt loop position

Sam Browne stud position

Belt loop position

20

0

0   20

Patterns

Photocopy enlargement
scale: 200%

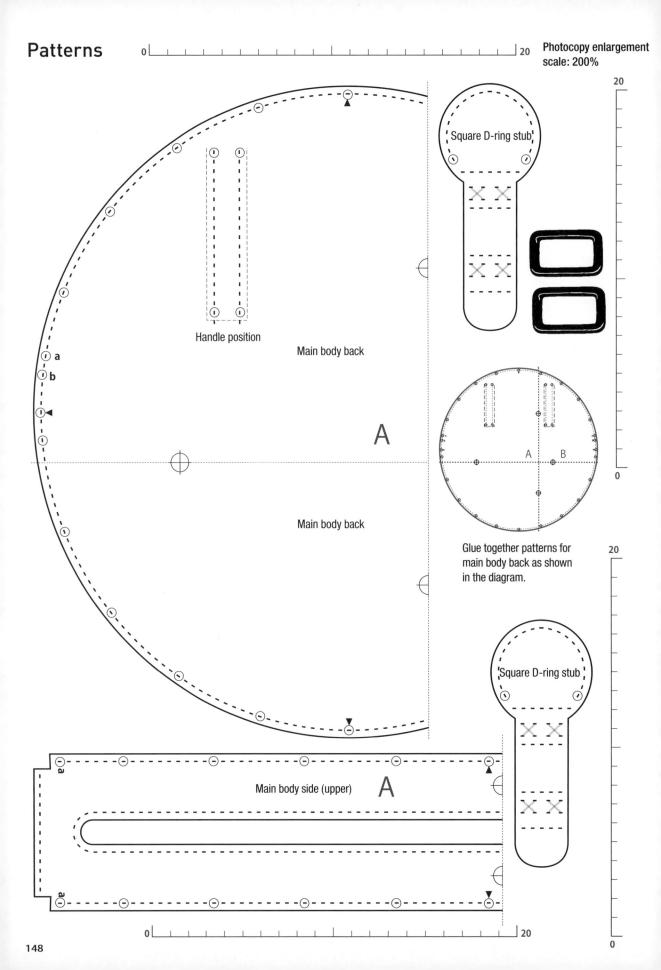

Handle position

Main body back

Main body back

Square D-ring stub

Square D-ring stub

A

A   B

Glue together patterns for
main body back as shown
in the diagram.

Main body side (upper)   A

Square D-ring stub

a

b

a

a

20

20

0

20

0

0

20

Patterns

Photocopy enlargement
scale: 200%

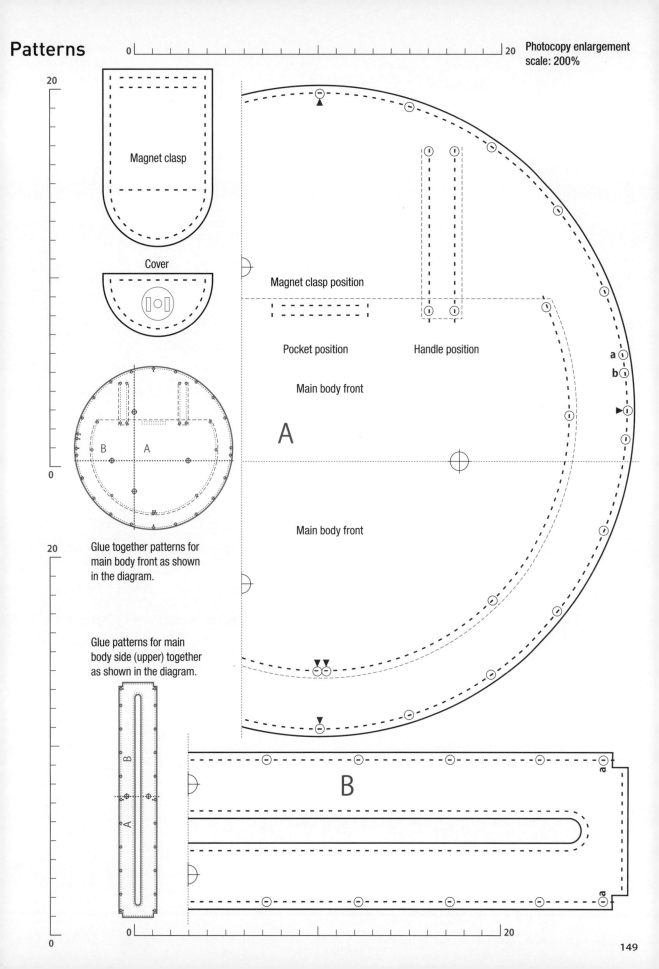

Magnet clasp

Cover

Magnet clasp position

Pocket position

Handle position

Main body front

A

Main body front

Glue together patterns for
main body front as shown
in the diagram.

Glue patterns for main
body side (upper) together
as shown in the diagram.

B

Patterns

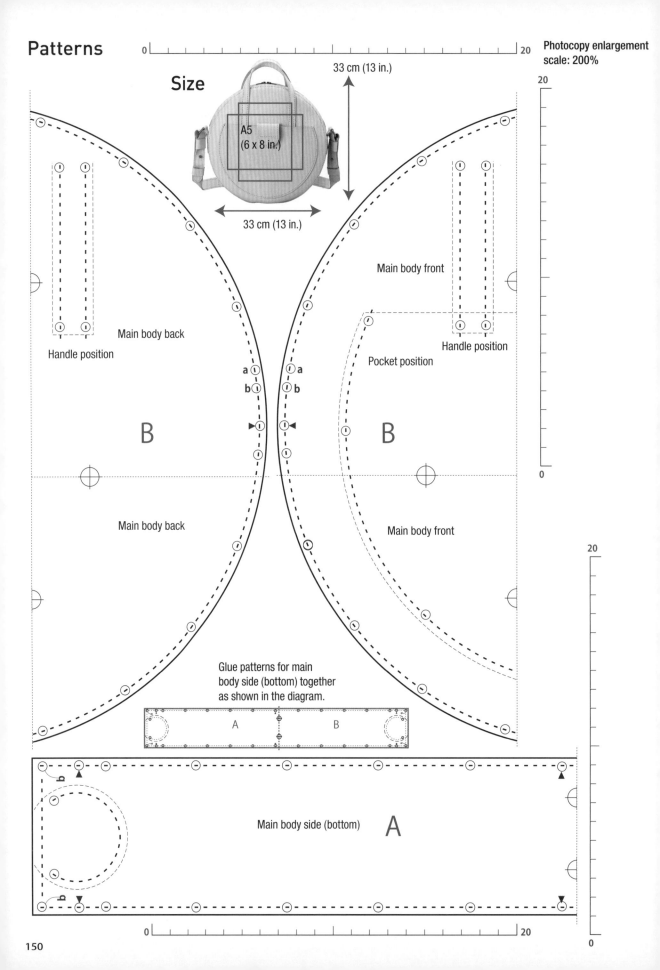

Size

33 cm (13 in.)

A5
(6 x 8 in.)

33 cm (13 in.)

Main body front

Main body back

Handle position

Pocket position

Handle position

a   a
b   b

B   B

Main body back

Main body front

Glue patterns for main
body side (bottom) together
as shown in the diagram.

A   B

Main body side (bottom)   A

0 ———————————————— 20

150

Patterns

0   20

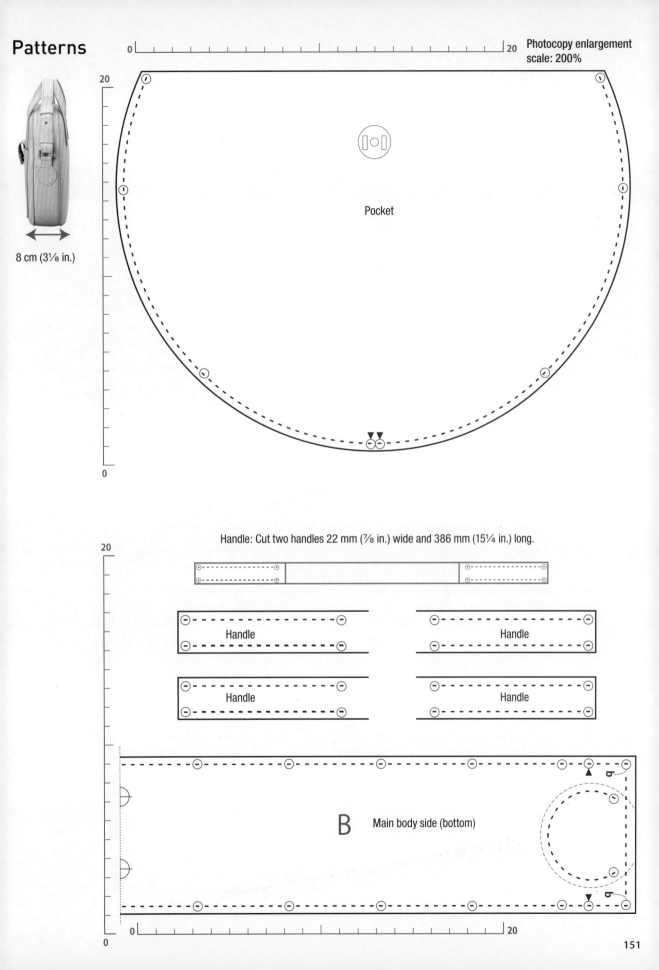

8 cm (3⅛ in.)

20

0

Pocket

Handle: Cut two handles 22 mm (⅞ in.) wide and 386 mm (15¼ in.) long.

Handle

Handle

Handle

Handle

B   Main body side (bottom)

0   20

Tanned Leather Bag No. 12
Small Handbag

Front

Side

Detail

Back

153

How To:

See "Creating a Simple Handle," p. 40–45.
See "Installing a Zipper," p. 50–51.
See "Three-Dimensional Bonding," p. 52.

Punching Stitching Holes and Cutting Leather

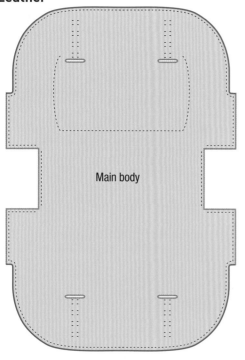

Main body

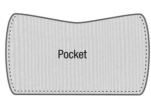

Pocket

- Apply burnishing agent to flesh side and edges marked with red lines.

- Transfer ○ marks on pattern to flesh side of the leather.

Handles

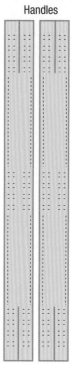

Creating Parts and Attaching to Main Body

1 Glue pocket to main body. Align stitching holes, then sew.

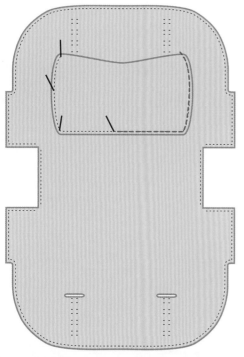

2 Moisten handle and fold in half. Then match marked stitching holes, glue, and sew.

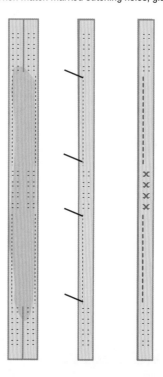

Creating Main Body

1 Mark zipper on flesh side of main body.
Glue one side of zipper tape to one side of main body edge, while aligning marks. Sew until outermost mark.

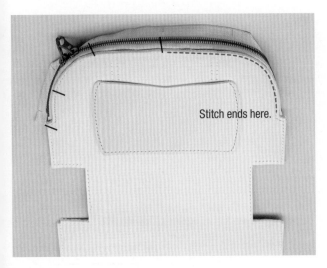

Stitch ends here.

2 Fold main body. For remaining edge, glue remaining zipper tape on main body edge while aligning marks. Then, sew to the outermost mark.

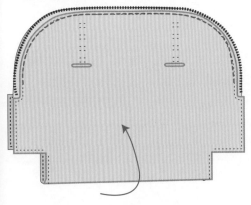

3 Unzip zipper and glue handle to main body. Align stitching holes, then sew.

Thread end of handle through the hole.

4 Glue side edges of main body, while aligning the stitching holes. Then, sew.

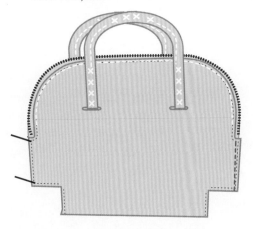

5 Unzip zipper. Glue end of zipper—which was left loose—then sew it on edge of bag opening.

6 Glue bottom edges of main body while aligning stitching holes. Then sew.

Bag bottom

Center hole on bottom of bag

Center hole on side of bag

Begin stitching from outermost point and then pass needle through center hole on bottom of bag, toward the center hole on side of bag.

Patterns

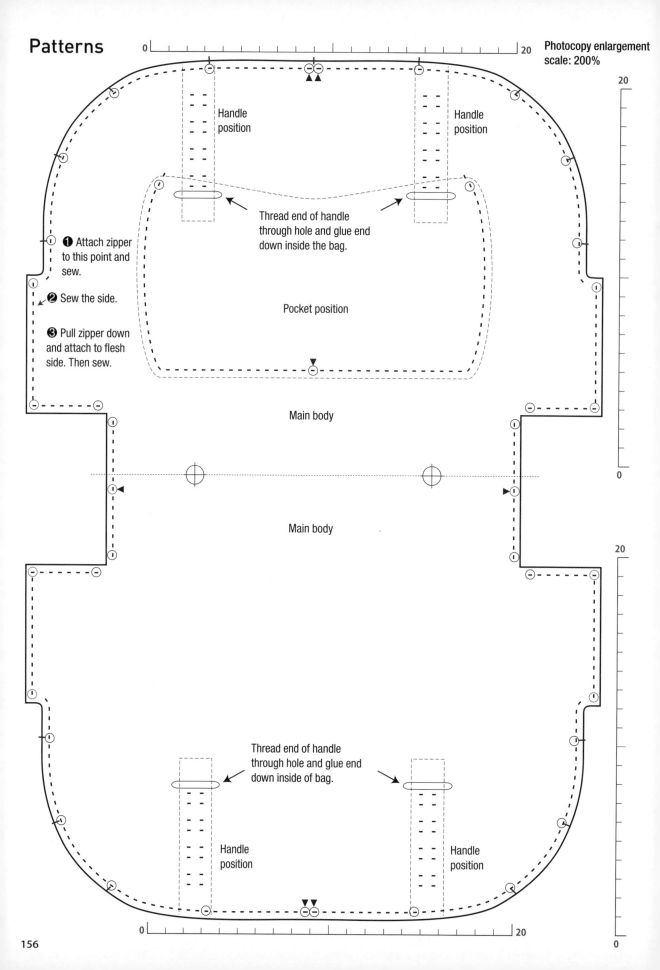

0 ————————— 20

20

Handle
position

Handle
position

Thread end of handle
through hole and glue end
down inside the bag.

❶ Attach zipper
to this point and
sew.

❷ Sew the side.

❸ Pull zipper down
and attach to flesh
side. Then sew.

Pocket position

Main body

Main body

20

0

20

Thread end of handle
through hole and glue end
down inside of bag.

Handle
position

Handle
position

0 ————————— 20

0

Patterns

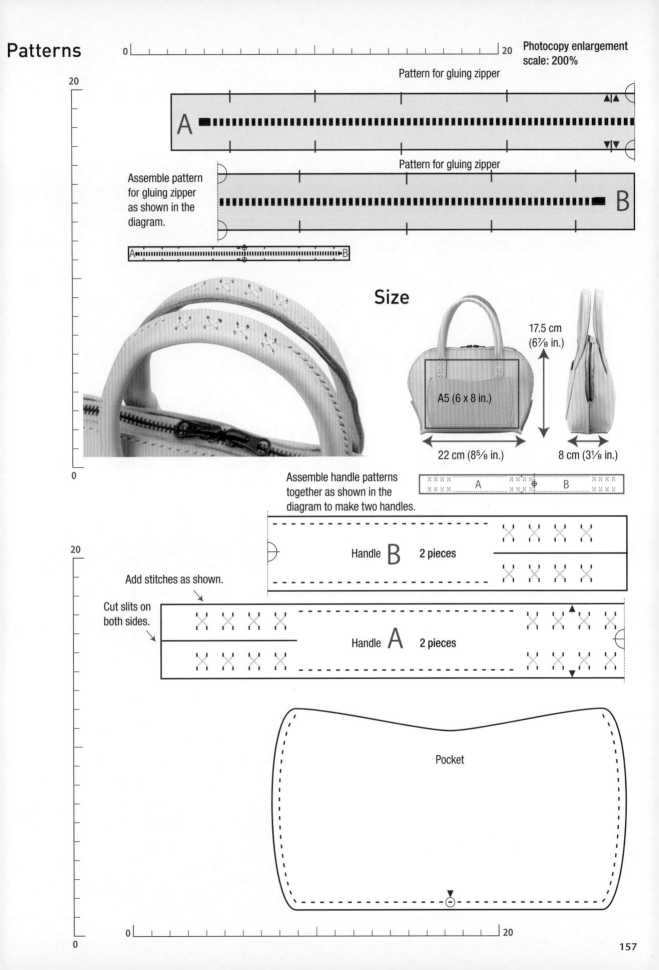

0 |_____| 20

Photocopy enlargement
scale: 200%

Pattern for gluing zipper

A

Assemble pattern
for gluing zipper
as shown in the
diagram.

Pattern for gluing zipper

B

A►◄------------------►B

Size

17.5 cm
(6⅞ in.)

A5 (6 x 8 in.)

22 cm (8⅝ in.)

8 cm (3⅛ in.)

Assemble handle patterns
together as shown in the
diagram to make two handles.

A ⊕ B

Handle **B** 2 pieces

Add stitches as shown.

Cut slits on
both sides.

Handle **A** 2 pieces

Pocket

Back

Side

Detail

How To:

Punching Stitching Holes and Cutting Leather

See "Creating a Simple Handle," p. 40–43.
  Two-ply and stitched along edges.
See "Installing Sam Browne Stud," p. 48
See "Installing a Zipper," p. 50–51.
See "Stitching Three Pieces of Leather, or More, at Once," p. 58.

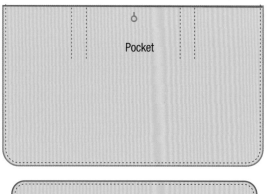

Pocket

- Apply burnishing agent along edges after stitching leather together.
- Transfer ○ marks on pattern to flesh side.

Handle

Back side   Pocket side

Zipper tabs

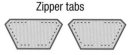

Main body front

Main body back

Creating Parts and Attaching to Main Body

1 Align main body, front and back, and glue on zipper.

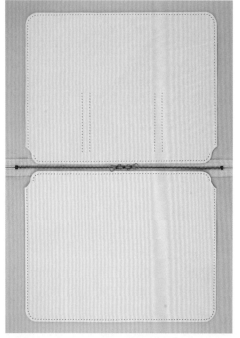

Glue and sew zipper tape ends up to marked points along the leather edge.

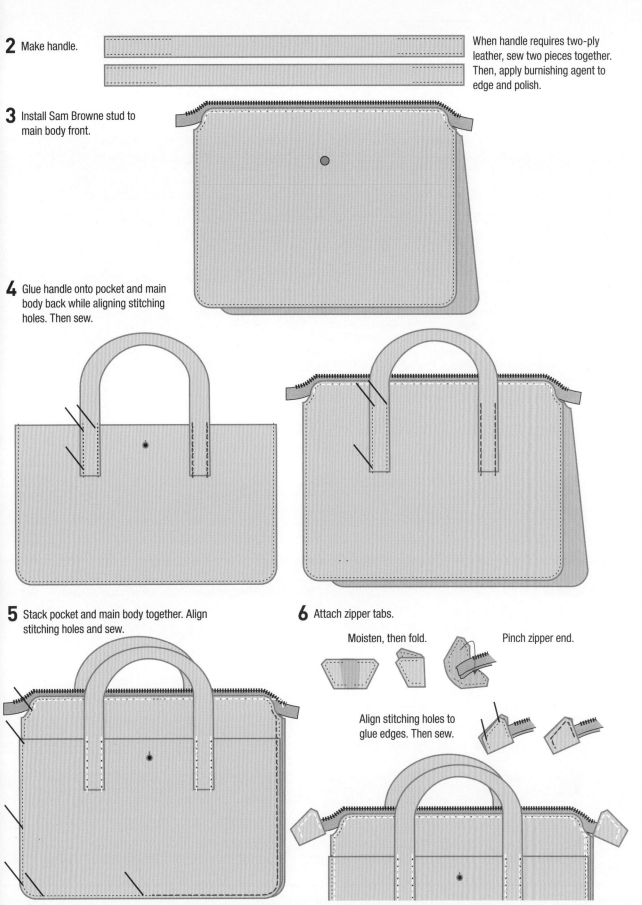

2 Make handle.

When handle requires two-ply leather, sew two pieces together. Then, apply burnishing agent to edge and polish.

3 Install Sam Browne stud to main body front.

4 Glue handle onto pocket and main body back while aligning stitching holes. Then sew.

5 Stack pocket and main body together. Align stitching holes and sew.

6 Attach zipper tabs.

Moisten, then fold.

Pinch zipper end.

Align stitching holes to glue edges. Then sew.

Patterns

0 |————————————————————————| 20

Photocopy enlargement scale: 200%

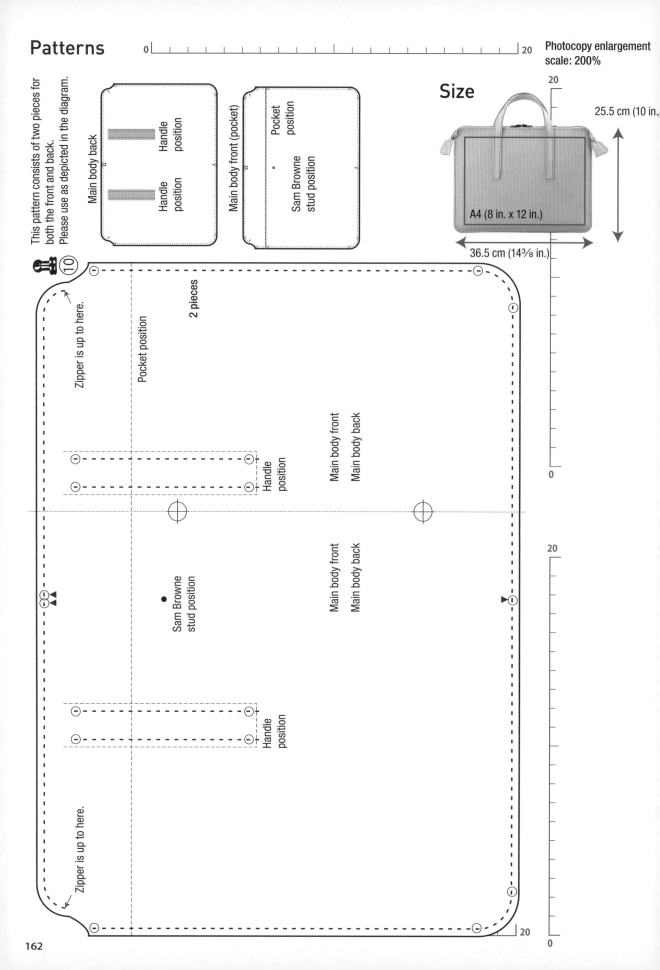

This pattern consists of two pieces for both the front and back. Please use as depicted in the diagram.

Main body back

Handle position

Handle position

Handle position

Main body front (pocket)

Pocket position

Sam Browne stud position

Size

20

25.5 cm (10 in.)

A4 (8 in. x 12 in.)

36.5 cm (14 3/8 in.)

Zipper is up to here.

Pocket position

2 pieces

Handle position

Main body front
Main body back

Main body front
Main body back

Sam Browne stud position

Handle position

Zipper is up to here.

20

0

20

0

20

20

0

Patterns

Photocopy enlargement
scale: 200%

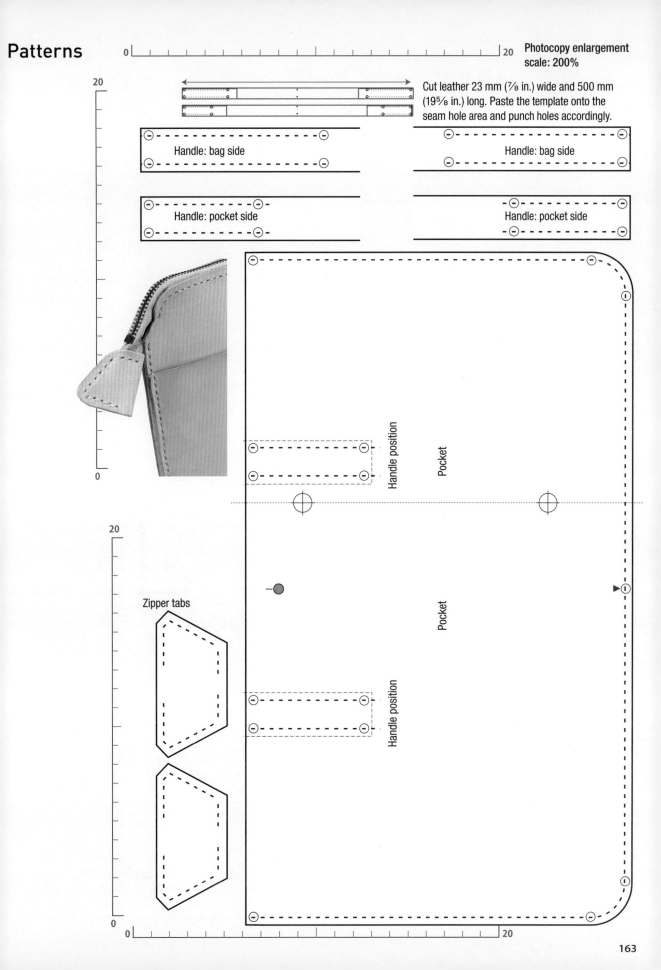

Cut leather 23 mm (⅞ in.) wide and 500 mm
(19⅝ in.) long. Paste the template onto the
seam hole area and punch holes accordingly.

Handle: bag side

Handle: bag side

Handle: pocket side

Handle: pocket side

Handle position

Pocket

Pocket

Handle position

Zipper tabs

Front

Back

Side

Detail

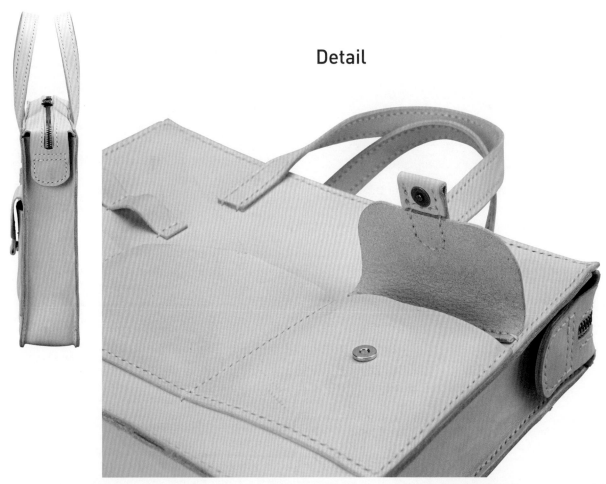

How To:

Punching Stitching Holes and Cutting Leather

See "Creating a Simple Handle," p. 40–45
Two-ply and stitched along edges.
See "Installing Magnet Clasp," p. 48.
See "Installing a Zipper," p. 50–51.
See "Three-Dimensional Bonding," p. 52.
See "Stitching Turned Edges," p. 53.

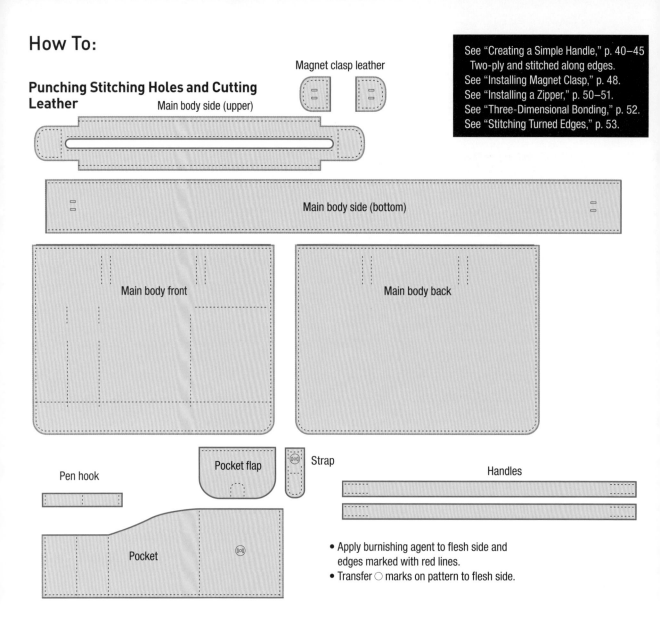

Magnet clasp leather

Main body side (upper)

Main body side (bottom)

Main body front

Main body back

Pen hook

Pocket flap

Strap

Handles

Pocket

- Apply burnishing agent to flesh side and edges marked with red lines.
- Transfer ○ marks on pattern to flesh side.

Creating Parts and Attaching to Main Body

1 Install zipper on main body side (upper).

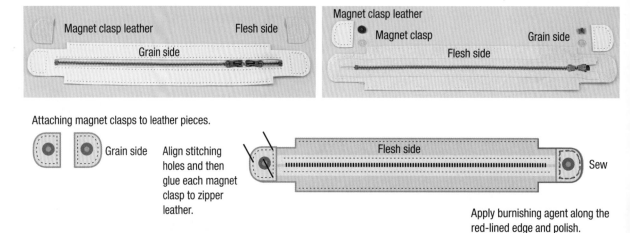

Magnet clasp leather   Flesh side

Grain side

Magnet clasp leather

Magnet clasp

Grain side

Flesh side

Attaching magnet clasps to leather pieces.

Grain side

Align stitching holes and then glue each magnet clasp to zipper leather.

Flesh side

Sew

Apply burnishing agent along the red-lined edge and polish.

2 Stitch handle.

★ If you want to add stitches around handle edge, sew as
 indicated on the diagram.

Don't stitch where handle
attaches to bag body.

Apply burnishing agent to edge
and polish.

3 Install magnet clasp.

Install magnet clasp
on leather.

Moisten and fold.
Align stitching holes
and then glue.

Align stitching holes
and glue magnet clasp
leather to pocket flap.
Then sew.

Install magnet
clasp on pocket.

4 Align stitching holes and glue parts on main body front.

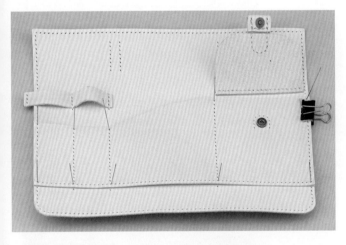

Sew

Sew end of pocket flap to
side seam.

5 Align stitching holes, then glue handles on main body
 front and back. Then sew.

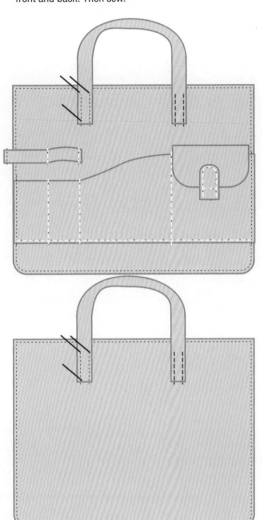

6 Install magnet clasp to both ends of the body side
 (bottom).

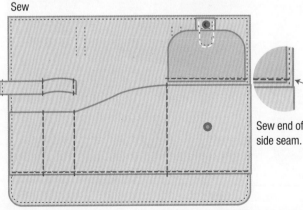

Creating Main Body

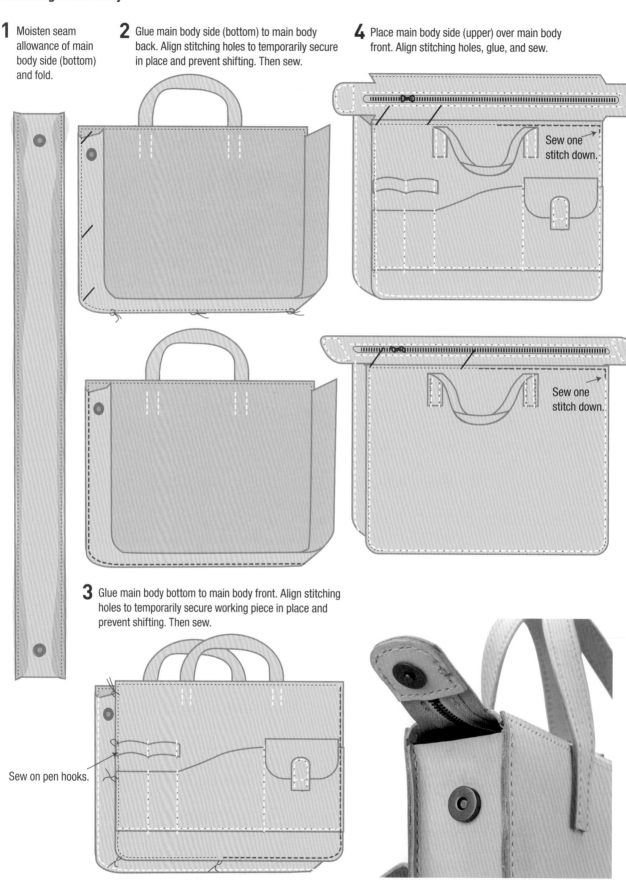

1 Moisten seam allowance of main body side (bottom) and fold.

2 Glue main body side (bottom) to main body back. Align stitching holes to temporarily secure in place and prevent shifting. Then sew.

3 Glue main body bottom to main body front. Align stitching holes to temporarily secure working piece in place and prevent shifting. Then sew.

Sew on pen hooks.

4 Place main body side (upper) over main body front. Align stitching holes, glue, and sew.

Sew one stitch down.

Sew one stitch down.

Patterns

Photocopy enlargement
scale: 200%

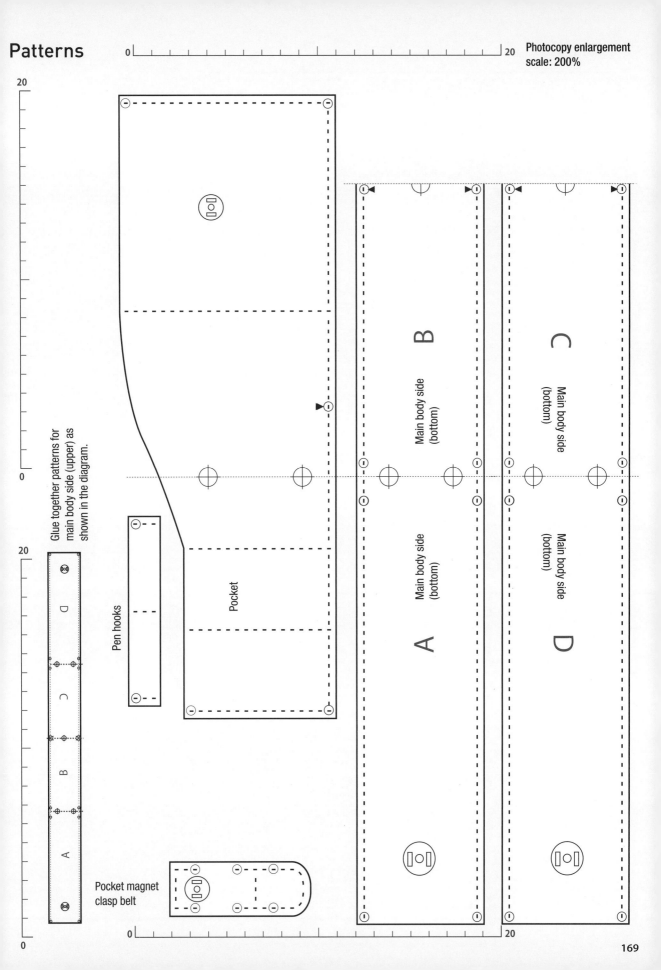

Glue together patterns for
main body side (upper) as
shown in the diagram.

Pen hooks

Pocket

B

C

Main body side
(bottom)

Main body side
(bottom)

A

D

Main body side
(bottom)

Main body side
(bottom)

Pocket magnet
clasp belt

A   B   C   D

Patterns

Photocopy enlargement
scale: 200%

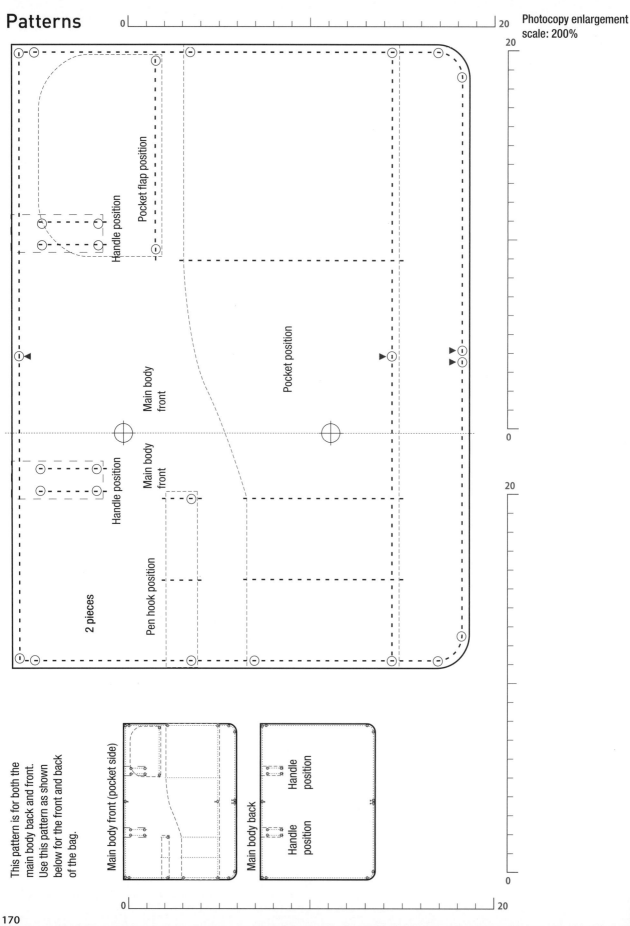

This pattern is for both the main body back and front. Use this pattern as shown below for the front and back of the bag.

2 pieces

Handle position

Pocket flap position

Handle position

Main body front

Pocket position

Main body front

Pen hook position

Main body front (pocket side)

Main body back

Handle position

Handle position

170

Patterns

Photocopy enlargement
scale: 200%

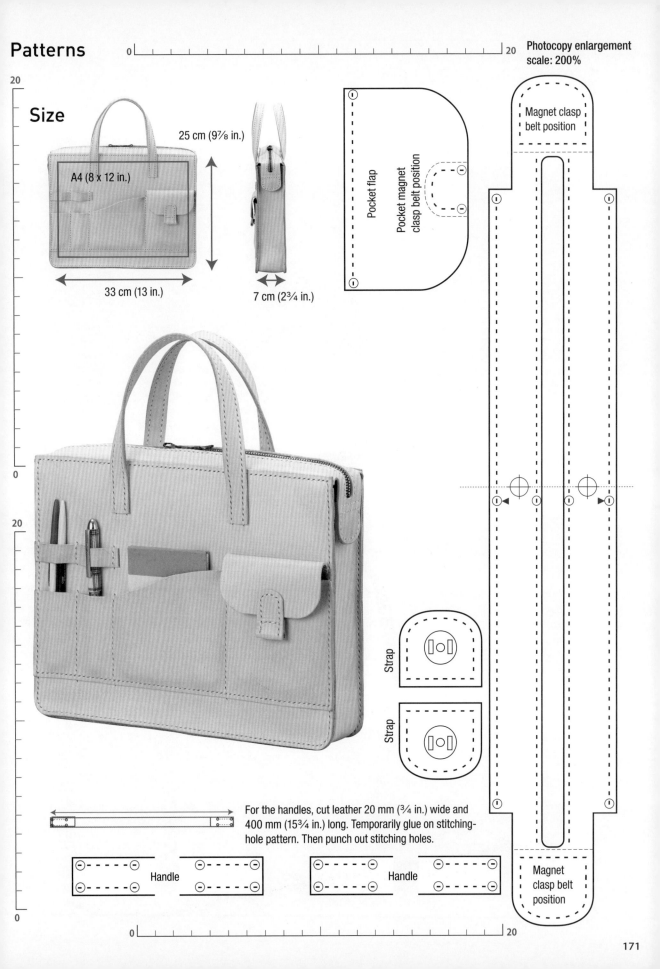

Size

A4 (8 x 12 in.)

25 cm (9⅞ in.)

33 cm (13 in.)

7 cm (2¾ in.)

Pocket flap

Pocket magnet clasp belt position

Magnet clasp belt position

Strap

Strap

For the handles, cut leather 20 mm (¾ in.) wide and 400 mm (15¾ in.) long. Temporarily glue on stitching-hole pattern. Then punch out stitching holes.

Handle

Handle

Magnet clasp belt position

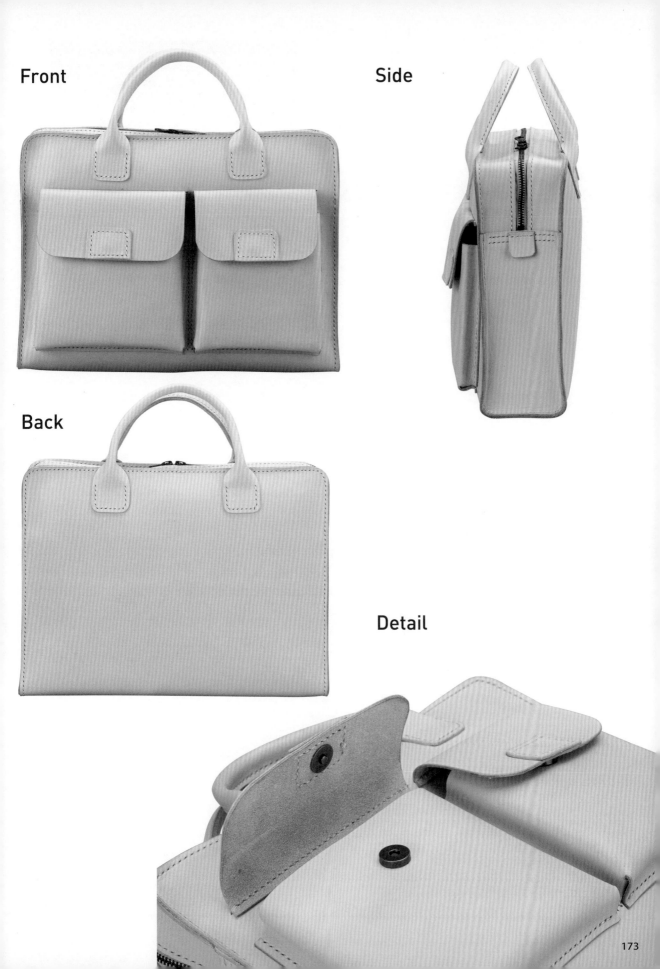

Front

Side

Back

Detail

How To:

See "Making a Folded Handle," p. 44.
See "Installing Magnet Clasp," p. 48.
See "Installing a Zipper," p. 50–51.
See "Three-Dimensional Bonding," p. 52.
See "Zipper Tab," p. 58. Attaching a tab aids with zipping/unzipping.

Punching Stitching Holes and Cutting Leather

- Apply burnishing agent to flesh side and edges marked with red lines.
- Transfer ○ marks on pattern to flesh side of leather.

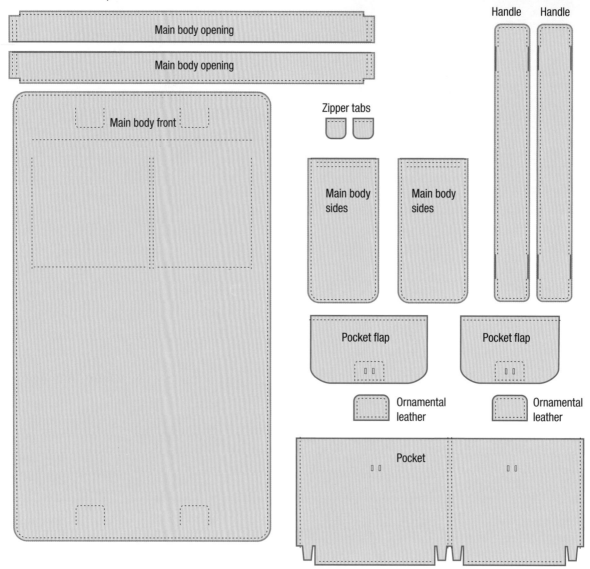

Creating Parts and Attaching to Main Body

1 Moisten handle and fold in half lengthwise. Align stitching holes up to marked position.

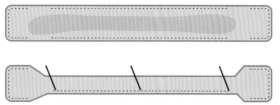

Sew.

Apply burnishing agent to edge and polish.

2 Glue zipper onto main body opening with a 13 mm (½ in.) gap. Then sew on zipper.

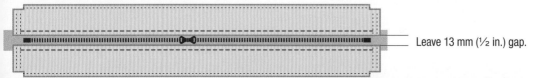

Leave 13 mm (½ in.) gap.

3 Glue main body opening to main body side. Align stitching holes, then sew.

Arrange zipper tabs and align stitching holes. Sew.

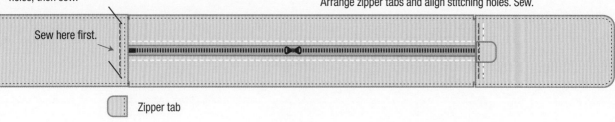

Sew here first.

Zipper tab

4 Attach magnet clasp on pocket flap.

Glue ornamental leather on pocket flap. Align stitching holes and sew.

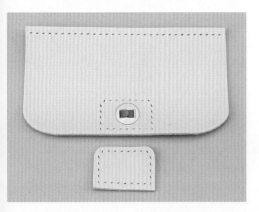

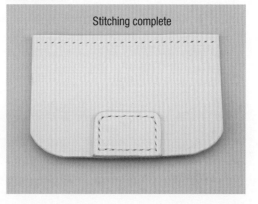

Stitching complete

5 Attach magnet clasp to pocket.

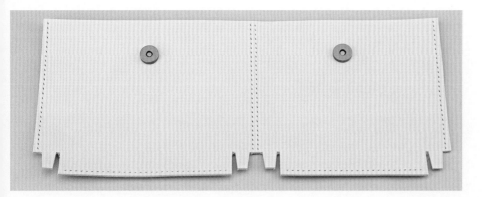

6 Glue pocket flap on main body. Align stitching holes and sew.

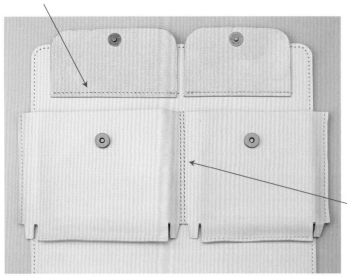

7 Moisten pocket.
Fold along gusset and shape for easy sewing.

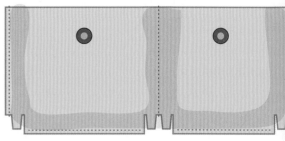

8 Glue pocket on main body while aligning central stitching holes along pocket center. Then sew.

9 Fold edges and corners. Glue while aligning stitching holes to temporarily secure in place and prevent shifting. Then sew on each pocket.

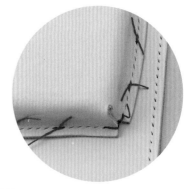

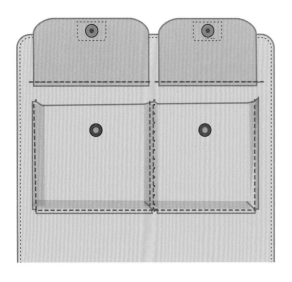

10 Align stitching holes and glue handles on main body. Sew.

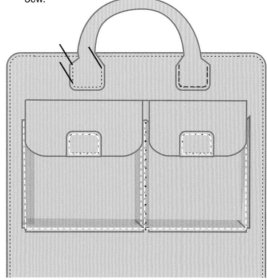

Creating Main Body

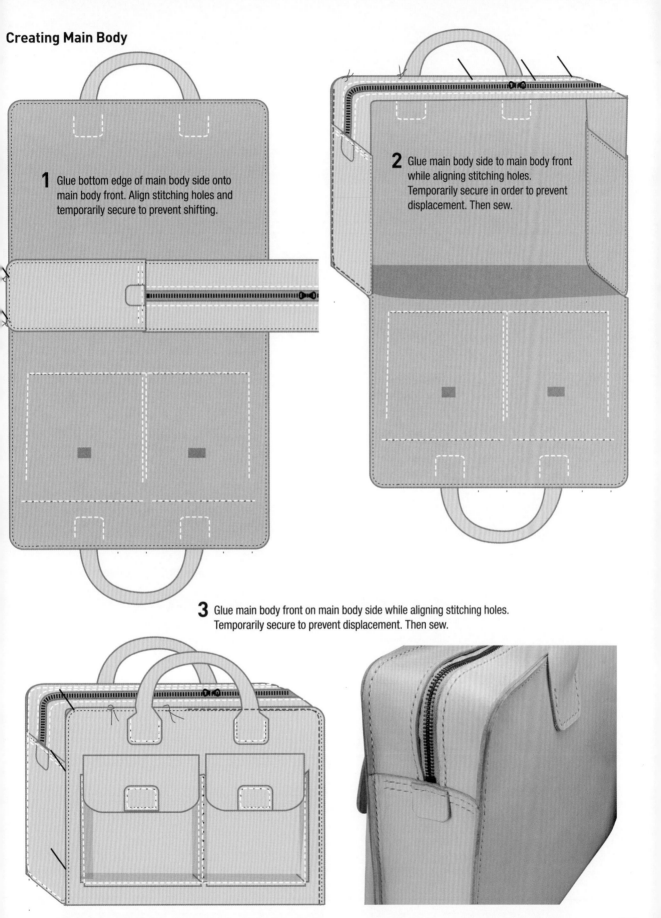

1 Glue bottom edge of main body side onto main body front. Align stitching holes and temporarily secure to prevent shifting.

2 Glue main body side to main body front while aligning stitching holes. Temporarily secure in order to prevent displacement. Then sew.

3 Glue main body front on main body side while aligning stitching holes. Temporarily secure to prevent displacement. Then sew.

Patterns

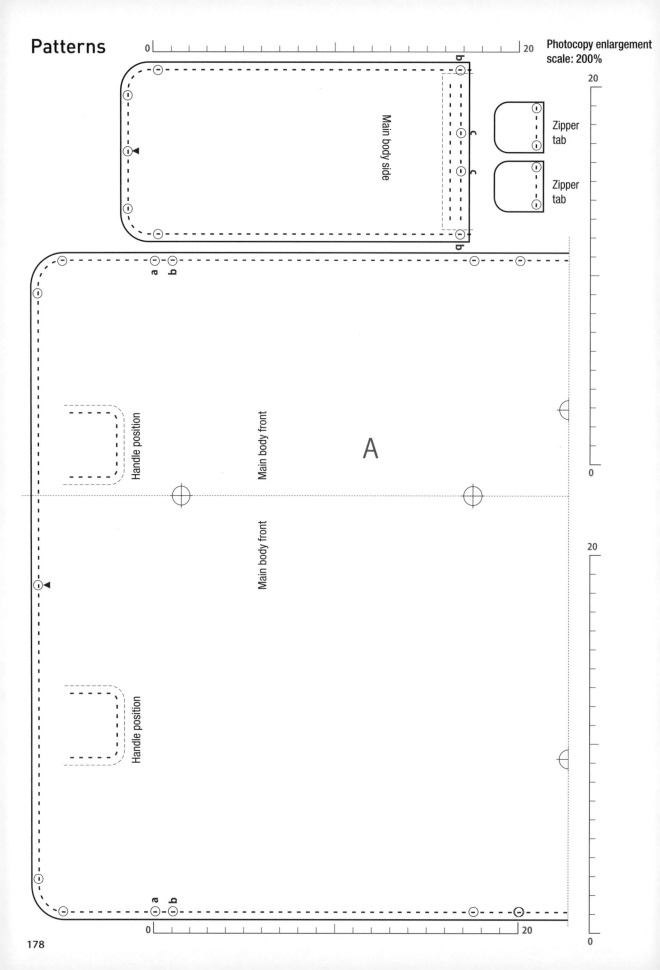

0 ⌞ 20

Photocopy enlargement
scale: 200%

Main body side

Zipper tab

Zipper tab

Handle position

Main body front

A

Main body front

Handle position

a b

a b

b

c

c

b

Patterns

Photocopy enlargement
scale: 200%

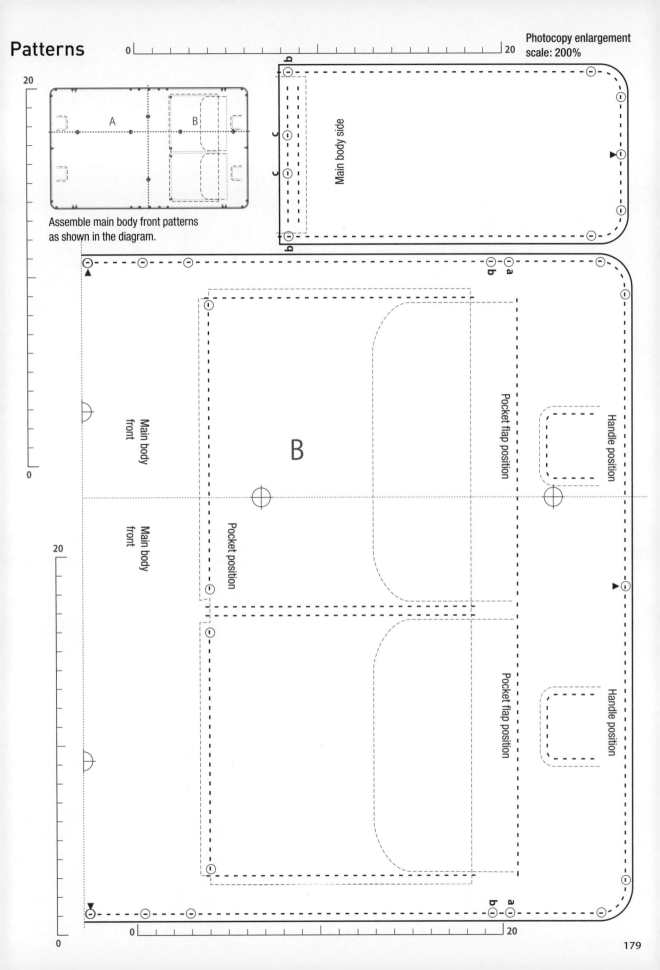

Assemble main body front patterns
as shown in the diagram.

Main body side

Main body
front

Main body
front

Pocket position

Pocket flap position

Pocket flap position

Handle position

Handle position

B

Patterns

Photocopy enlargement
scale: 200%

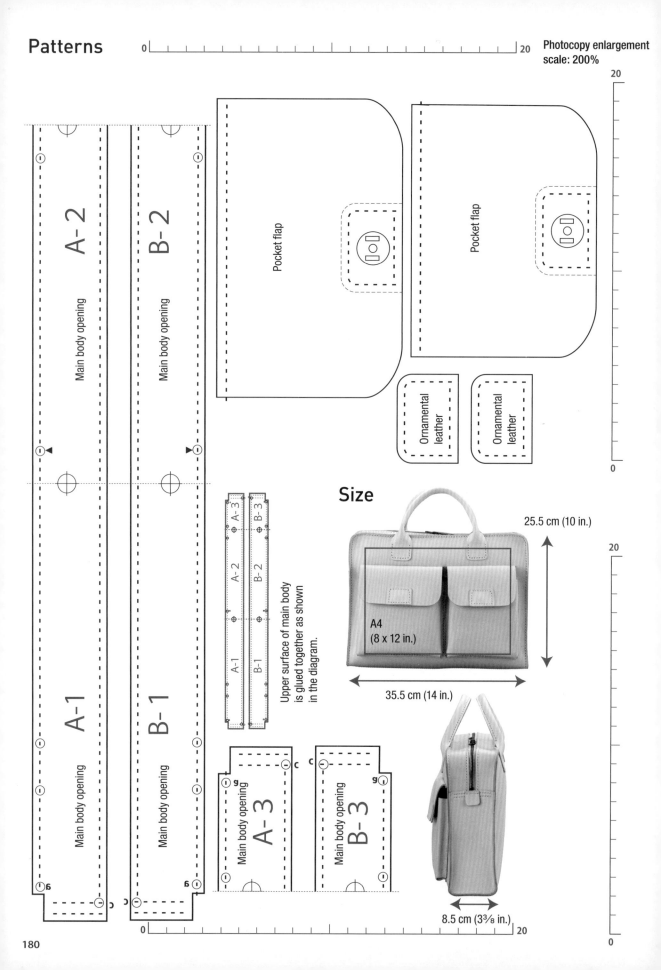

A–2

Main body opening

B–2

Main body opening

Pocket flap

Pocket flap

Ornamental leather

Ornamental leather

A–1

Main body opening

B–1

Main body opening

A–3 B–3

A–2 B–2

A–1 B–1

Upper surface of main body
is glued together as shown
in the diagram.

Main body opening

A–3

Main body opening

B–3

Size

25.5 cm (10 in.)

A4
(8 x 12 in.)

35.5 cm (14 in.)

8.5 cm (3⅜ in.)

0 |——————————————| 20

Patterns

Photocopy enlargement
scale: 200%

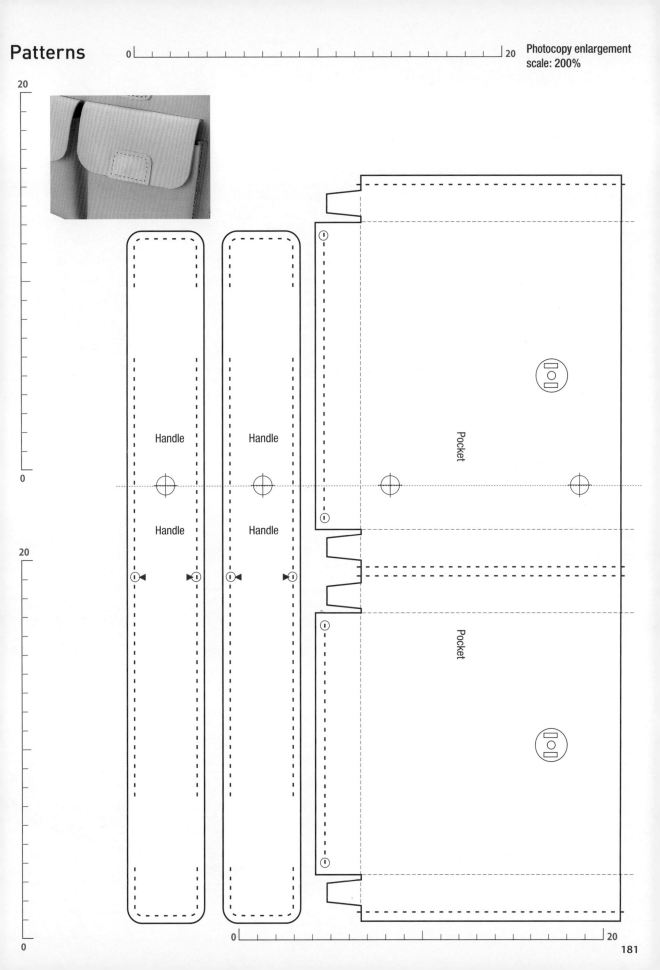

Handle

Handle

Handle

Handle

Pocket

Pocket

Front

Side

How To:

Punching Stitching Holes and Cutting Leather

- Apply burnishing agent to flesh side and edges marked with red lines.
- Transfer ○ marks on pattern to flesh side of leather.

See "How to Make Shoulder Strap and Pattern," p. 40–47.
   Stitch as specified in diagram.
See "Creating a Simple Handle," p. 40–43.
   2-ply, stitched along edges.
See "Attaching Buckle," p. 46–47.
See "Installing Sam Browne Stud," p. 48
See "Installing a Zipper," p. 50–51.
See "Three-Dimensional Bonding," p. 52.
See "Stitching Three Pieces of Leather, or More, at Once," p. 58.

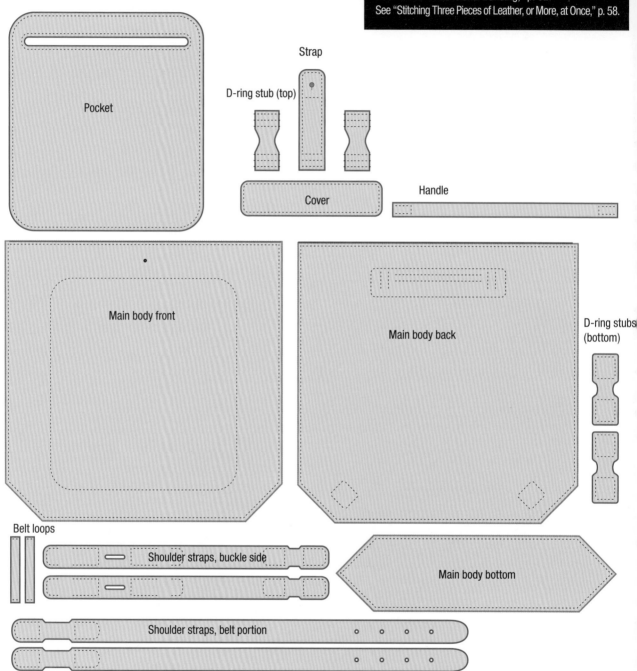

Creating Parts and Attaching to Main Body

1 Install zipper on pocket.

★ Please choose zipper orientation that allows for easy opening.

Zipper installed

2 Install Sam Browne stud on main body front. Glue pocket on main body. Align stitching holes. Then sew.

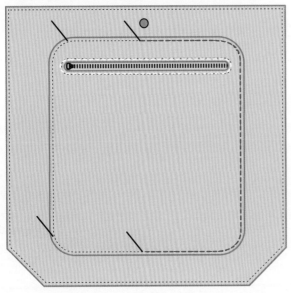

3 Moisten both D-ring stub—attached on top and bottom of backpack—and thread with a D-ring. Fold in half. Align stitch holes and glue.

4 Align stitching holes. Glue on strap, D-ring stubs, and handle, on the main body back. Then sew everything on.

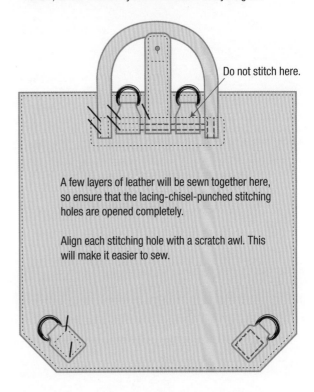

Do not stitch here.

A few layers of leather will be sewn together here, so ensure that the lacing-chisel-punched stitching holes are opened completely.

Align each stitching hole with a scratch awl. This will make it easier to sew.

5 Glue on cover while aligning stitching holes. Then sew.

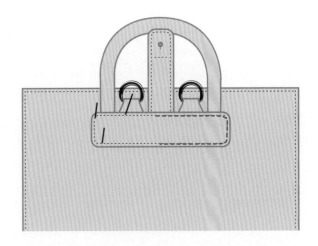

Creating Main Body

1 Install zipper while leaving a gap between front and back of main body.

2 Glue main body bottom to main body front and back. Align stitching holes and temporarily secure working piece in place to prevent shifting. Then sew.

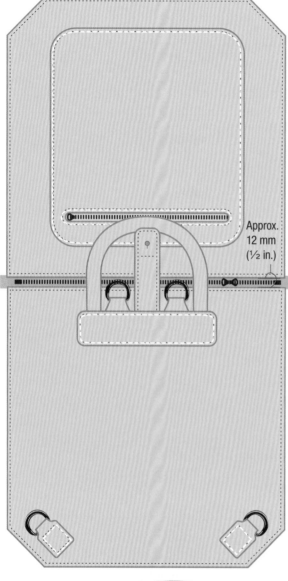

Approx. 12 mm (½ in.)

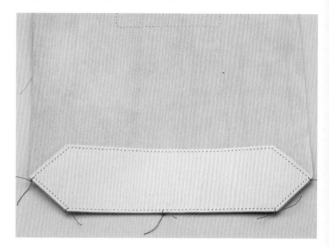

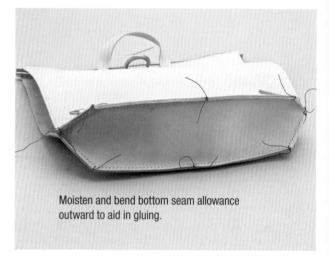

Moisten and bend bottom seam allowance outward to aid in gluing.

3 Glue main body bottom to main body front and back. Align stitching holes and temporarily secure working piece in place to prevent shifting. Then sew.

Fold end of zipper tape and glue down.

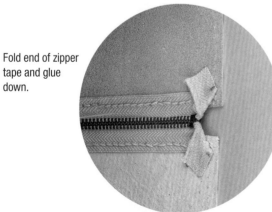

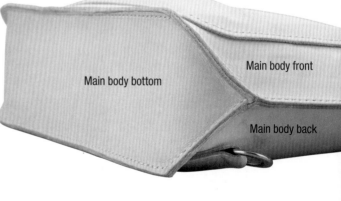

Main body bottom

Main body front

Main body back

Patterns

Photocopy enlargement
scale: 200%

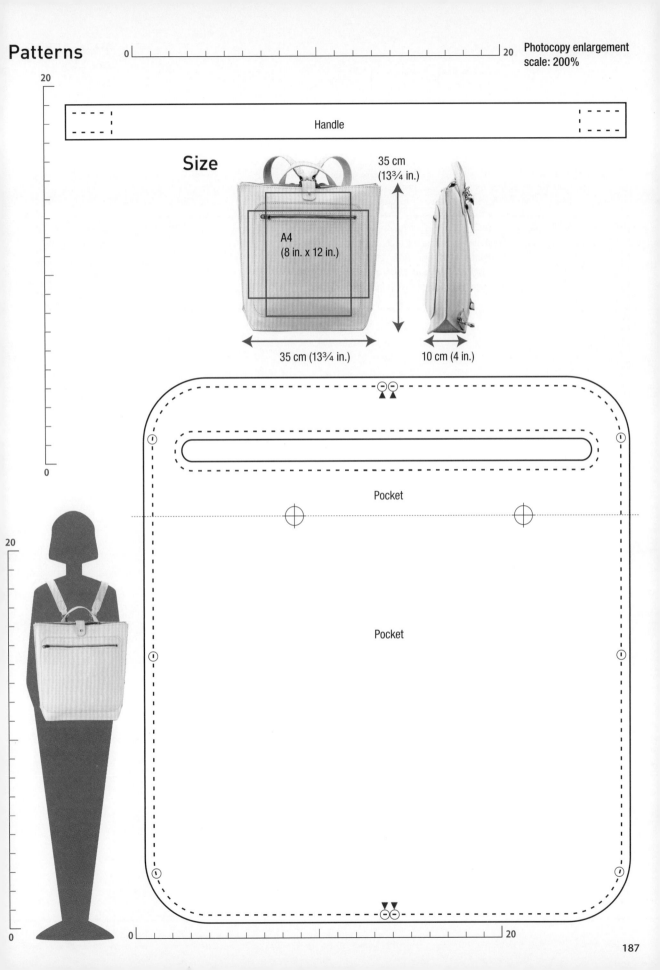

20

Handle

Size

35 cm
(13¾ in.)

A4
(8 in. x 12 in.)

35 cm (13¾ in.)

10 cm (4 in.)

0

20

Pocket

Pocket

0

20

0

0 ⊢────────────────────┤ 20

Patterns

Photocopy enlargement scale: 200%

Glue patterns for main body front together as shown in diagram.

A   B

20

After completion, we recommend that you determine the Sam Browne stud (base) position by aligning it with the strap. Confirm hole positions and then punch them out.

Pocket position

Main body front

0

A

Main body front

20

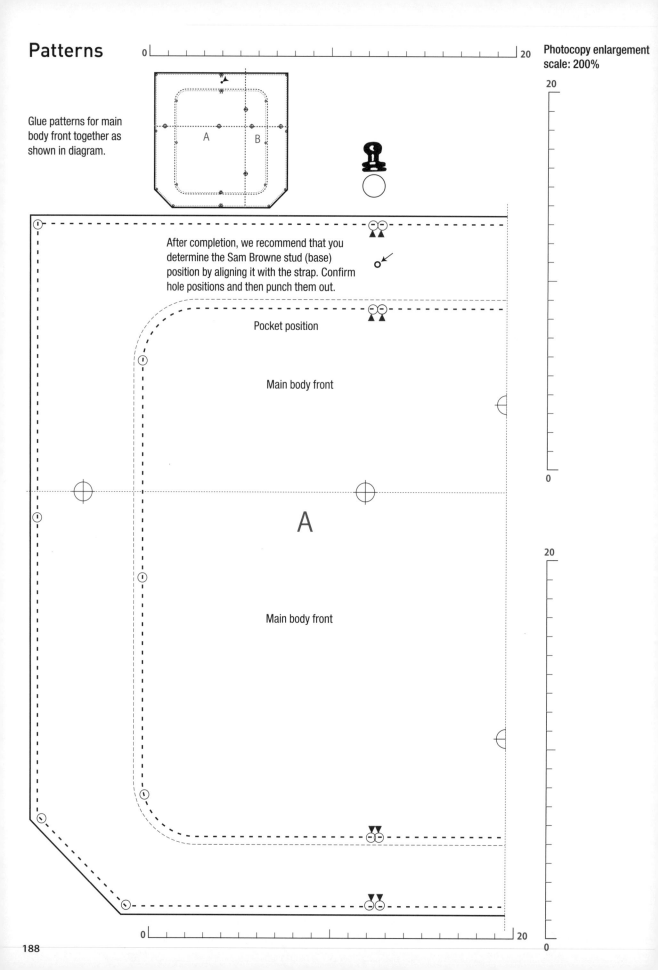

0 |————————————————| 20

0

Patterns

Photocopy enlargement
scale: 200%

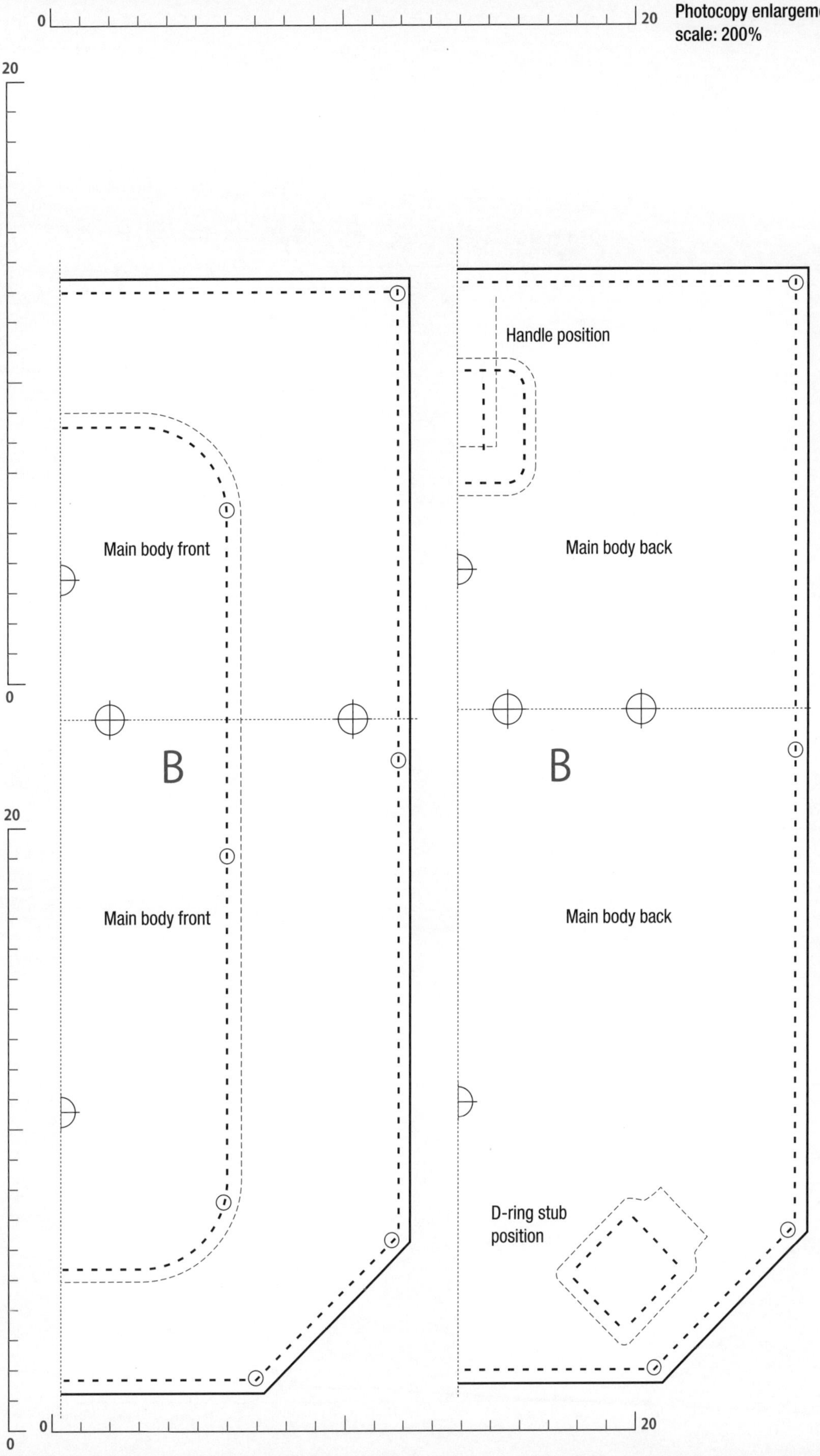

20

Main body front

B

20

Main body front

0

Handle position

Main body back

B

Main body back

D-ring stub
position

0   20

Patterns

0 |————————————————| 20

Photocopy enlargement scale: 200%

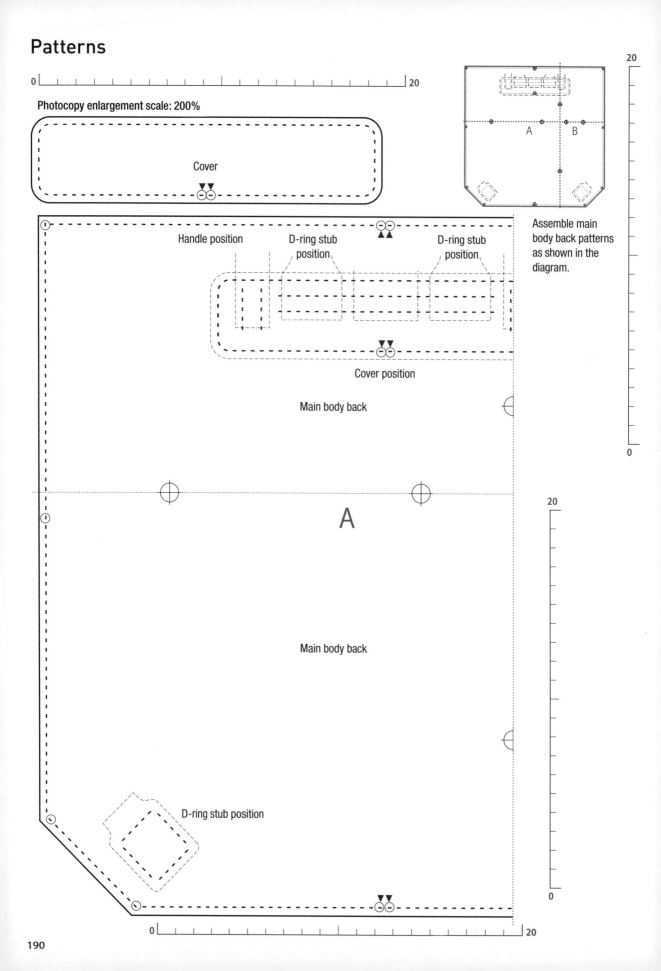

Cover

Handle position

D-ring stub position

D-ring stub position

Cover position

Main body back

Main body back

A

D-ring stub position

Assemble main body back patterns as shown in the diagram.

A   B

20

0

20

0

20

0

0 |————————————————| 20

Patterns

Photocopy enlargement
scale: 200%

Assemble main
body bottom
patterns as
shown in the
diagram.

A   B

A   Main body bottom

Main body bottom   B

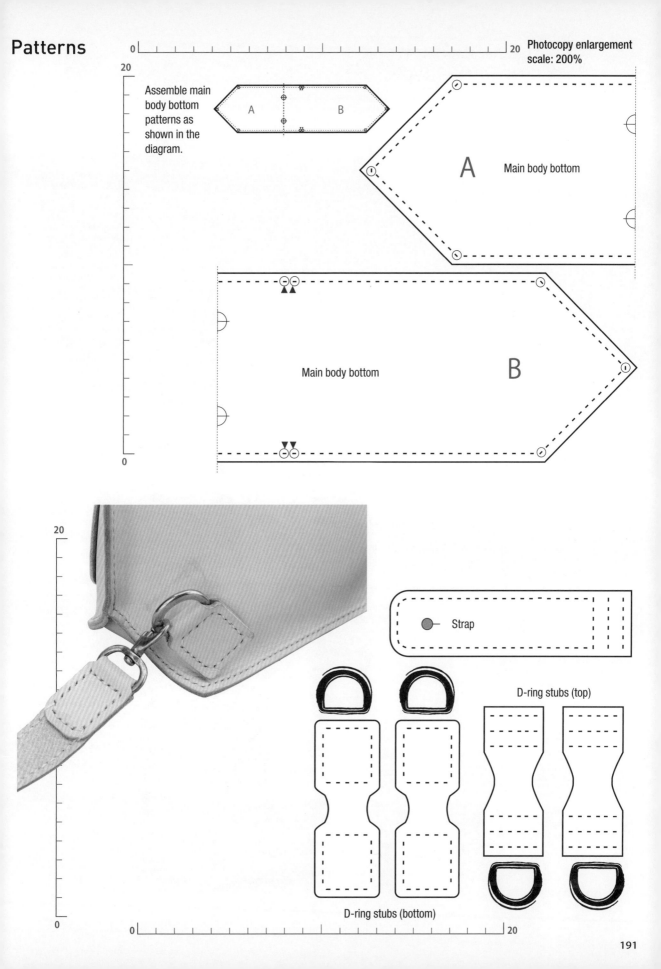

Strap

D-ring stubs (top)

D-ring stubs (bottom)

Backpack Satchel Type

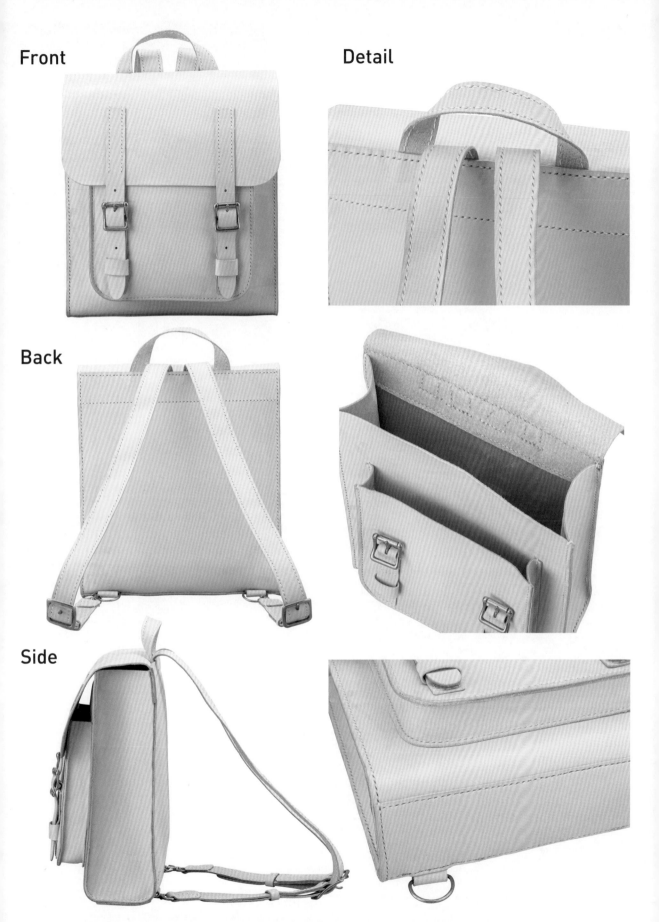

Front

Detail

Back

Side

How To:

Punching Stitching Holes and Cutting Leather

See "How to Make Shoulder Strap and Pattern," p. 40–47.
  Stitch as specified in the diagram.
See "Creating a Simple Handle," p. 40–43.
  Stitched along edges.
See "Attaching Buckle," p. 46–47.
See "Three-Dimensional Bonding," p. 52.
See "Stitching Three Pieces of Leather, or More, at Once," p. 58.

• Apply burnishing agent to flesh side of leather and edges marked with red lines.
• Transfer ○ marks on pattern to flesh side of the leather.

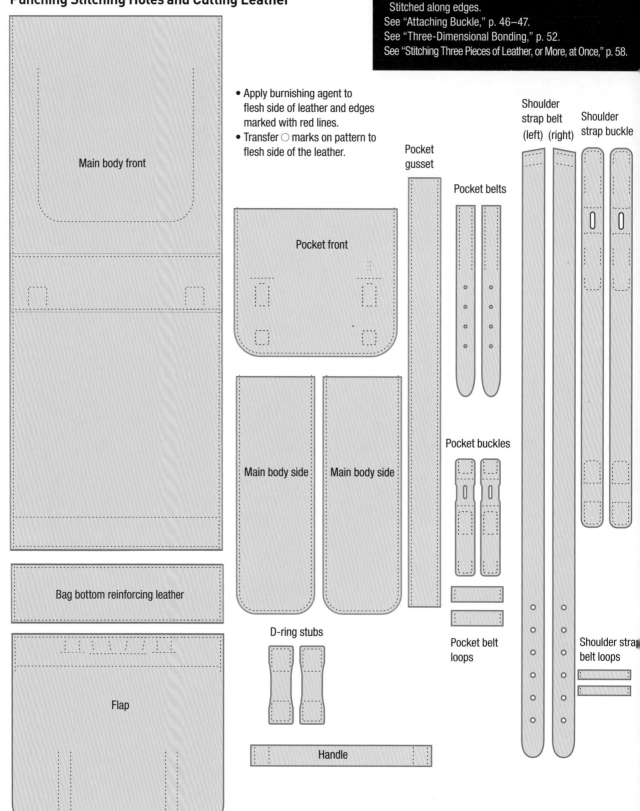

Main body front

Bag bottom reinforcing leather

Flap

Pocket front

Main body side

Main body side

D-ring stubs

Handle

Pocket gusset

Pocket belts

Pocket buckles

Pocket belt loops

Shoulder strap belt (left) (right)

Shoulder strap buckle

Shoulder strap belt loops

Creating Parts and Attaching to Main Body

1 Fold belt loop in half and sew along center.

Pass buckle and belt loop through lower part of buckle belt. Align stitching holes with pocket. Glue and sew.

2 Attach gusset to pocket.
Bond edges while aligning stitching holes. Temporarily secure to prevent displacement, then then sew.

3 Attach pocket to main body.
Glue while aligning stitching holes to temporarily secure in place and prevent shifting.

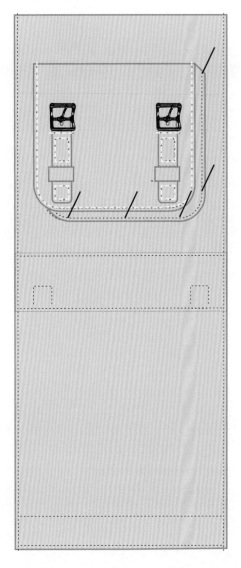

It's easier to sew if you moisten and bend the gusset seam allowance beforehand.

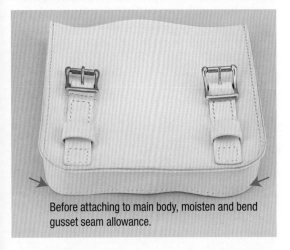

Before attaching to main body, moisten and bend gusset seam allowance.

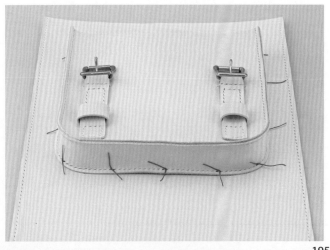

Creating Main Body

4 Lay handle and shoulder strap belt on flap while aligning stitching holes. Glue on flap and stitch.

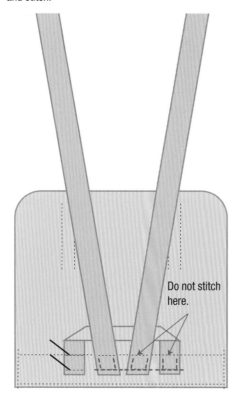

Do not stitch here.

5 Lay main body on flap. Align stitching holes and glue main body onto flap. Temporarily secure to prevent displacement. Then sew.

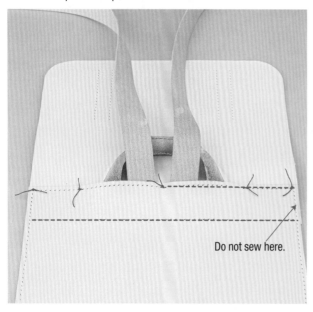

Do not sew here.

6 Install D-ring.

Moisten D-ring stub and insert D-ring, then fold D-ring stub.
Align stitching holes. Then glue.

Attach D-ring stub to main body by aligning stitching holes. Glue and then sew.

Do not stitch here.

Attach bag bottom reinforcement piece to main body by aligning stitching holes. Glue and then sew.

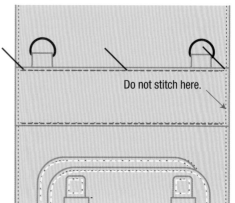

Do not stitch here.

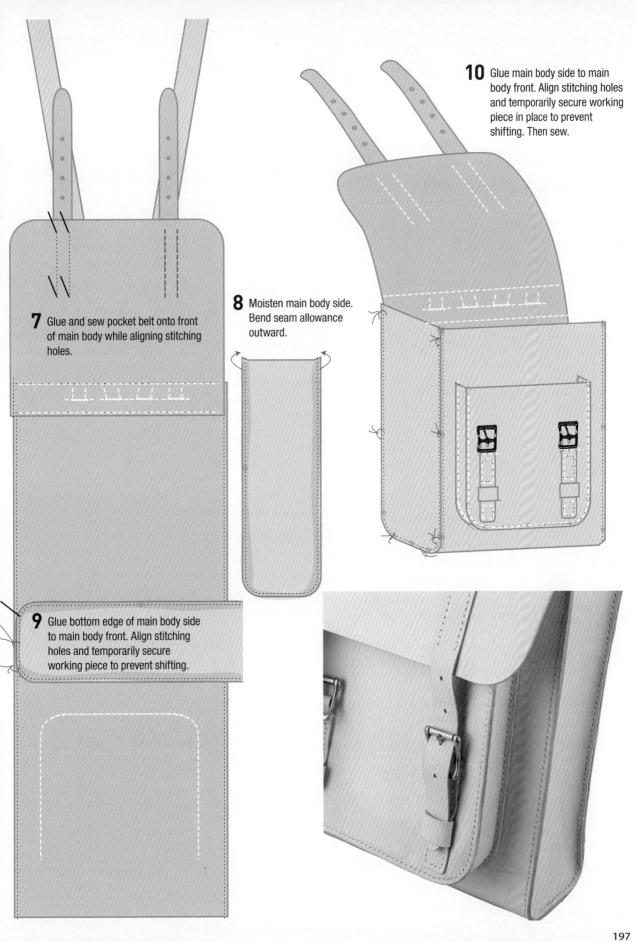

7 Glue and sew pocket belt onto front of main body while aligning stitching holes.

8 Moisten main body side. Bend seam allowance outward.

9 Glue bottom edge of main body side to main body front. Align stitching holes and temporarily secure working piece to prevent shifting.

10 Glue main body side to main body front. Align stitching holes and temporarily secure working piece in place to prevent shifting. Then sew.

Patterns

0 |_____| 20

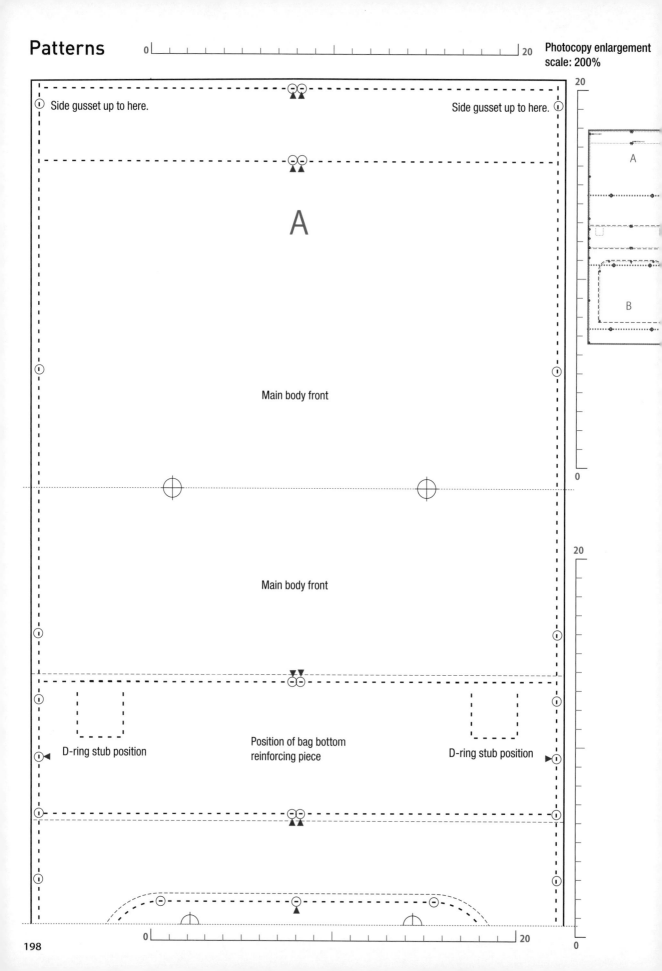

Side gusset up to here.

Side gusset up to here.

A

Main body front

Main body front

D-ring stub position

Position of bag bottom
reinforcing piece

D-ring stub position

0 |_____| 20

Patterns

Photocopy enlargement
scale: 200%

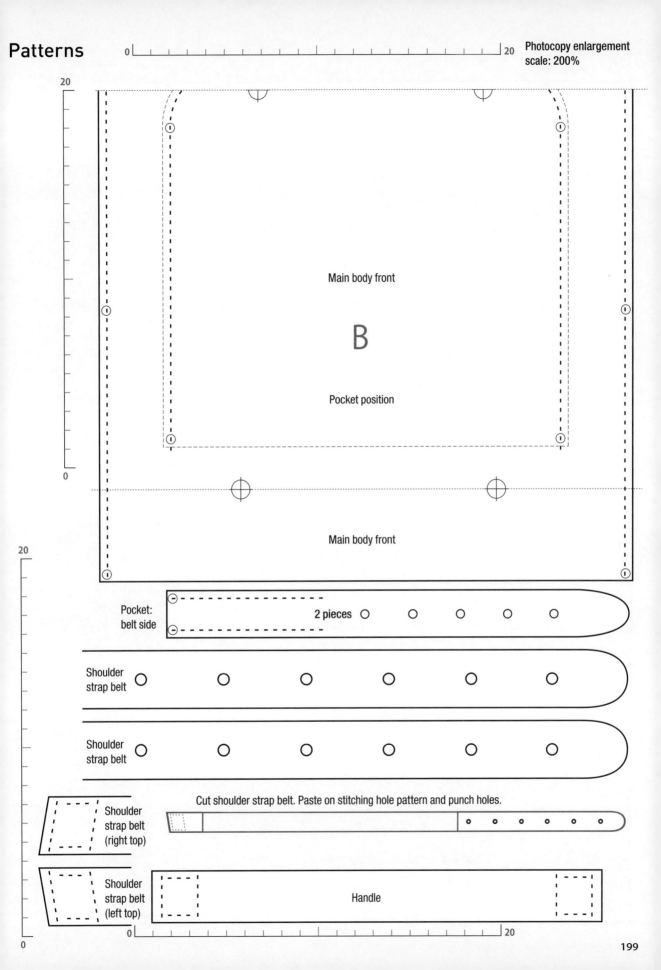

Main body front

B

Pocket position

Main body front

Pocket:
belt side

2 pieces

Shoulder
strap belt

Shoulder
strap belt

Cut shoulder strap belt. Paste on stitching hole pattern and punch holes.

Shoulder
strap belt
(right top)

Shoulder
strap belt
(left top)

Handle

Patterns

**Photocopy enlargement
scale: 200%**

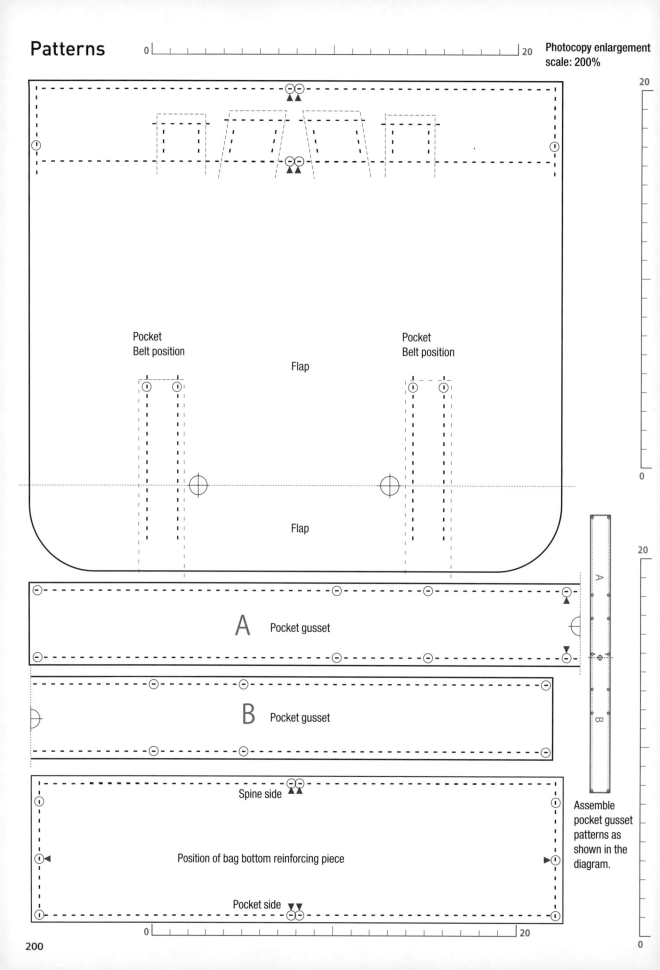

Pocket
Belt position

Pocket
Belt position

Flap

Flap

A Pocket gusset

B Pocket gusset

Spine side

Position of bag bottom reinforcing piece

Pocket side

A

B

Assemble
pocket gusset
patterns as
shown in the
diagram.

20

0

0   20

20

0

Patterns

20

2 pieces

Belt loop

Pocket
Buckle belt

D-ring stub

2 pieces

2 pieces

0

Pocket front

Pocket
Buckle belt
position

Pocket
Buckle belt
position

Assemble
patterns for
main body side
as shown in the
diagram. Make
two pieces.

32.5 cm
(12¾ in.)

A4 (8 x 12 in.)

A

B

A

Main body side

Main body side

2 pieces

2 pieces

B

28.5 cm (11¼ in.)

9.5 cm (3¾ in.)

20

0

0 |_____| 20

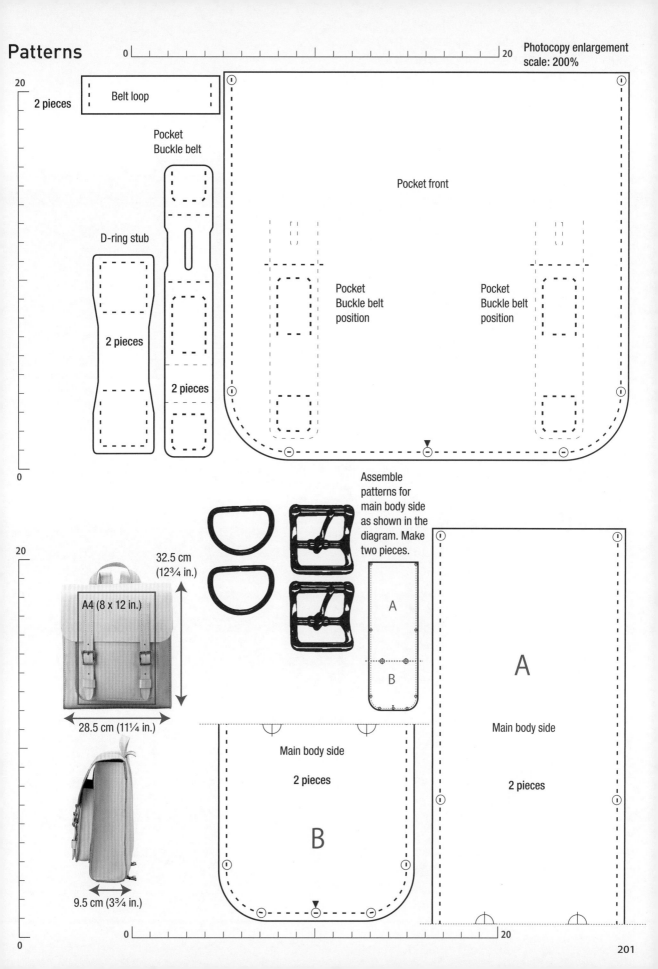

Tanned Leather Bag No. 18
Backpack Briefcase Type

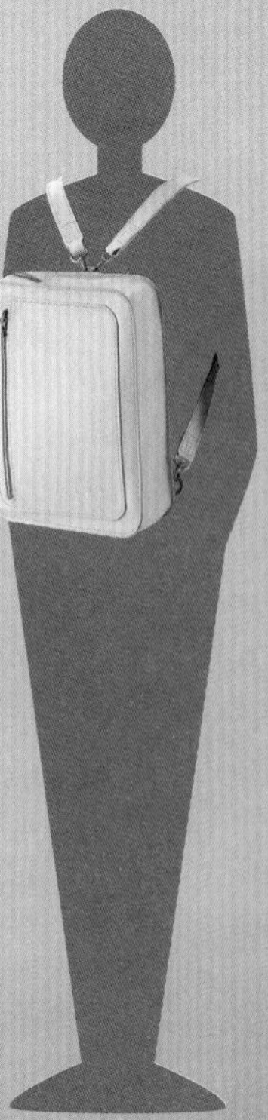

Front

Side

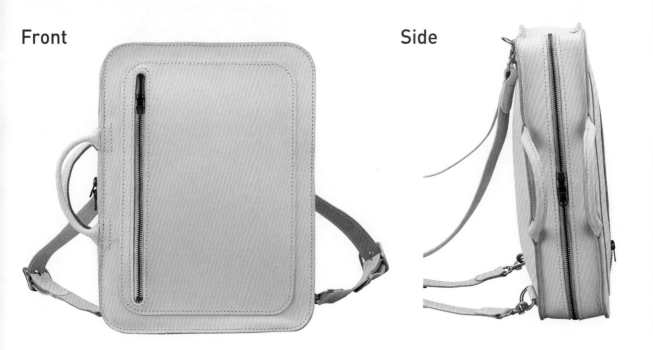

Back

Detail

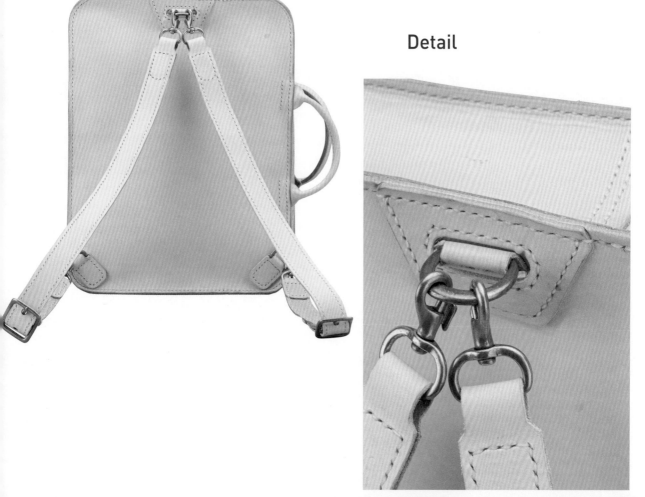

How To:

Punching Stitching Holes and Cutting Leather

See "How to Make Shoulder Strap and Pattern," p. 40–47.
  Stitched along edges.
See "Making a Folded Handle," p. 44.
See "Attaching Buckle," p. 46–47.
See "Installing a Zipper," p. 50–51.
See "Three-Dimensional Bonding," p. 52.
See "Stitching Three Pieces of Leather, or More, at Once," p. 58.
See "Zipper Tab," p. 58, attaching a tab aids zipping/unzipping.

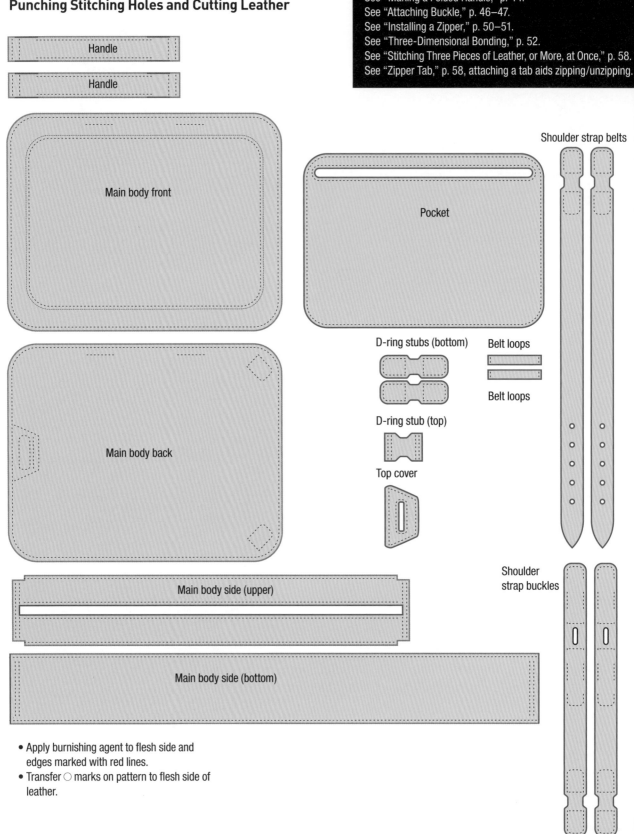

Handle

Handle

Main body front

Pocket

Shoulder strap belts

Main body back

D-ring stubs (bottom)

Belt loops

Belt loops

D-ring stub (top)

Top cover

Main body side (upper)

Shoulder strap buckles

Main body side (bottom)

- Apply burnishing agent to flesh side and edges marked with red lines.
- Transfer ○ marks on pattern to flesh side of leather.

Creating Parts and Attaching to Main Body

1 Glue and sew zipper onto pocket.

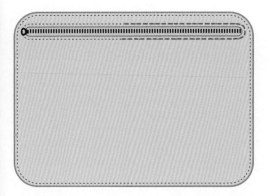

2 Align stitching holes. Glue pocket on main body front, and then sew.

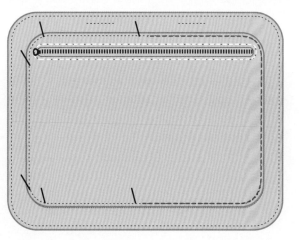

3 Install D-ring.

Moisten D-ring stub (top) and D-ring stub (bottom). Insert a D-ring into each belt, then fold stubs.

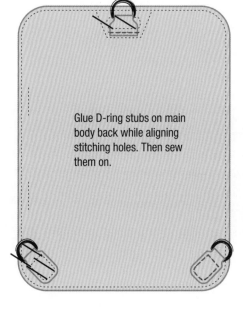

Glue D-ring stubs on main body back while aligning stitching holes. Then sew them on.

Do not stitch here.

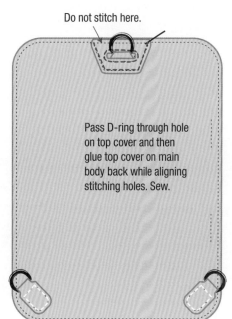

Pass D-ring through hole on top cover and then glue top cover on main body back while aligning stitching holes. Sew.

4 Make handles.

Moisten handle and fold it in half.

Align stitching holes in order to glue edges. Then sew.

Apply burnishing agent and polish edges.

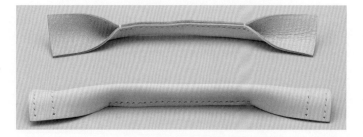

5 Attach handles to flesh side of main body front and back.
Align stitching holes in order to glue the edges. Then sew.

Do not stitch here.

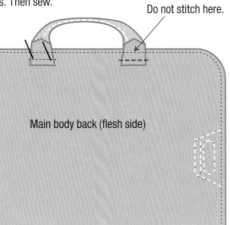

Main body back (flesh side)

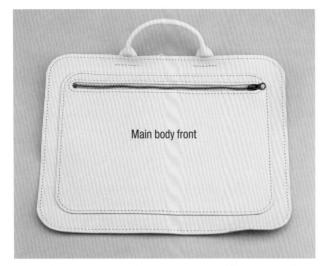

Main body front

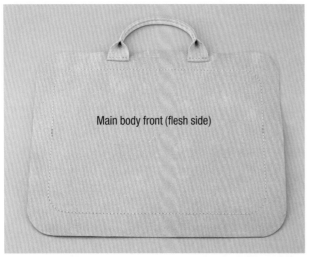

Main body front (flesh side)

6 Place end of main body side (top) over end of main body side (bottom). Align stitching holes and glue. Sew.

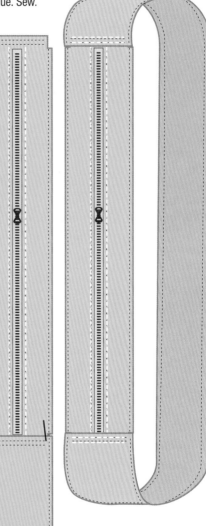

Moisten seam allowance and bend outward.

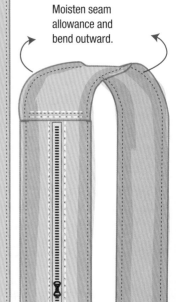

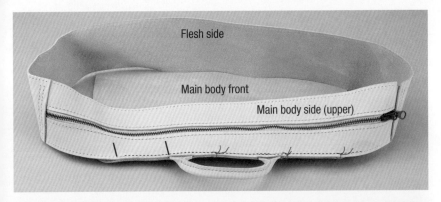

Flesh side

Main body front

Main body side (upper)

Creating Main Body

1 Glue main body side on main body back while aligning stitching holes. It's easier to glue if we align holes while moving out from the center mark.
Temporarily secure to prevent displacement. Then sew.

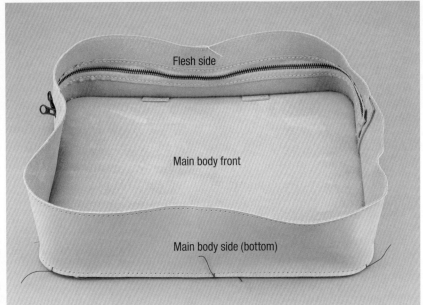

Flesh side

Main body front

Main body side (bottom)

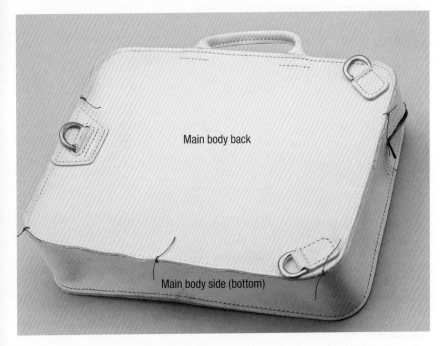

2 Put main body back on working piece (step 6) and glue edges together while aligning stitching holes.
Temporarily secure to prevent displacement, then sew.

Main body back

Main body side (bottom)

Patterns

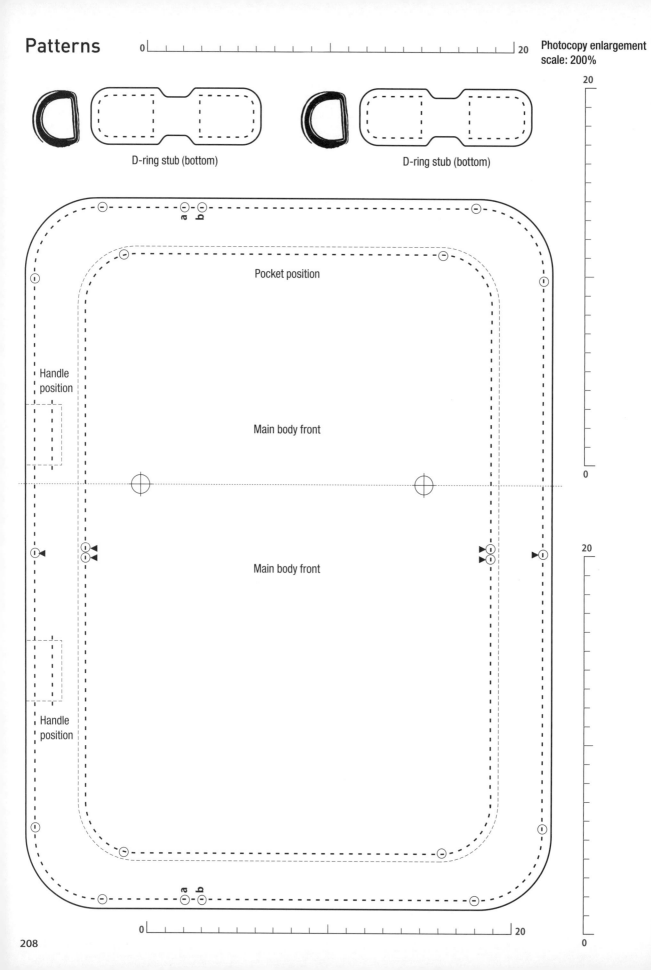

D-ring stub (bottom)

D-ring stub (bottom)

Pocket position

Handle position

Main body front

Main body front

Handle position

Patterns

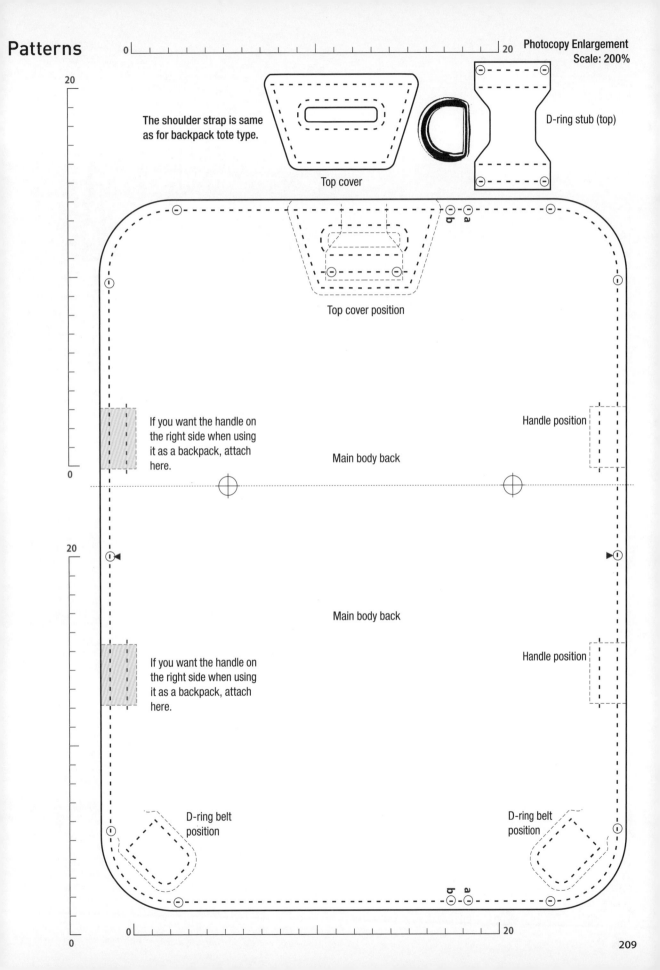

The shoulder strap is same
as for backpack tote type.

Top cover

D-ring stub (top)

Top cover position

If you want the handle on
the right side when using
it as a backpack, attach
here.

Main body back

Handle position

Main body back

If you want the handle on
the right side when using
it as a backpack, attach
here.

Handle position

D-ring belt
position

D-ring belt
position

Patterns

Photocopy enlargement
scale: 200%

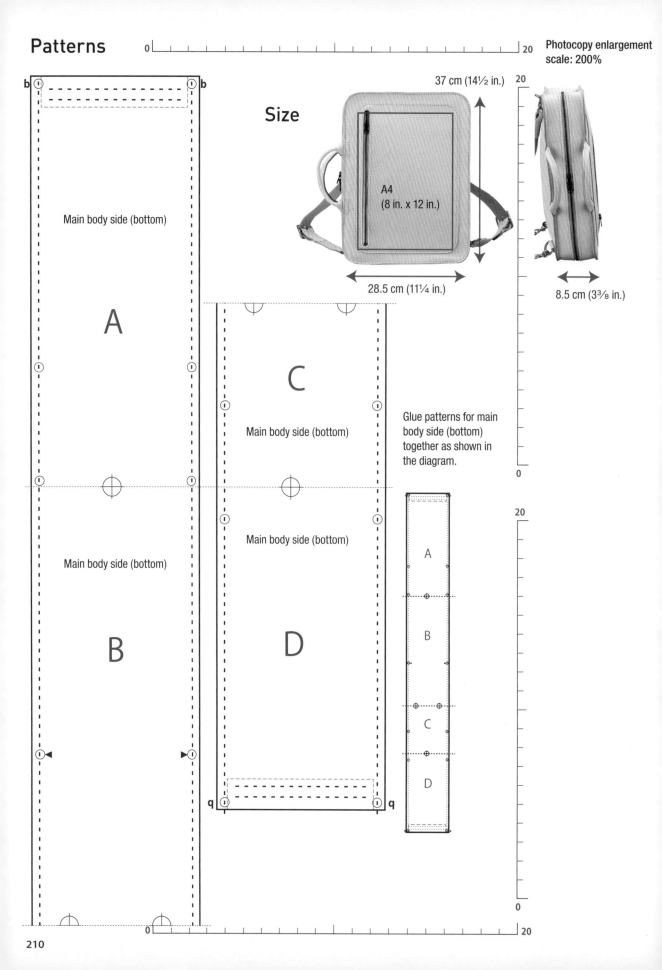

b ⓘ ⓘ b

Main body side (bottom)

A

ⓘ ⓘ

Size

37 cm (14½ in.)

20

A4
(8 in. x 12 in.)

28.5 cm (11¼ in.)

8.5 cm (3⅜ in.)

C

Main body side (bottom)

ⓘ ⓘ

Glue patterns for main
body side (bottom)
together as shown in
the diagram.

0

⊕   ⊕

Main body side (bottom)

ⓘ ⓘ

Main body side (bottom)

20

A

Main body side (bottom)

B

ⓘ ◄   ►ⓘ

D

C

B   D

q ⓘ ⓘ q

0

0

20

210

Patterns

Photocopy enlargement
scale: 200%

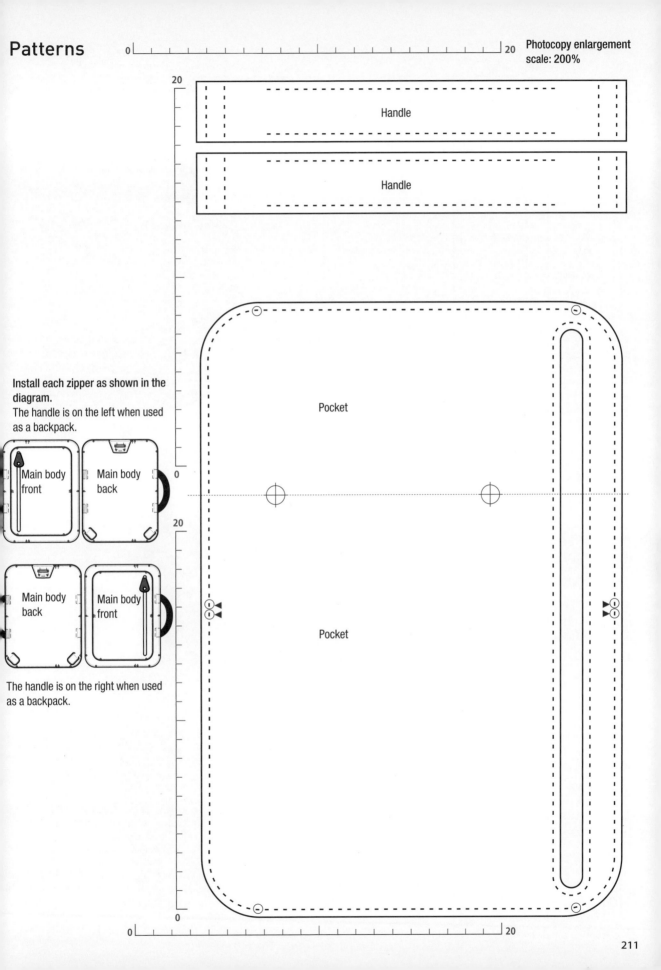

Handle

Handle

Install each zipper as shown in the diagram.
The handle is on the left when used as a backpack.

Main body front

Main body back

Main body back

Main body front

The handle is on the right when used as a backpack.

Pocket

Pocket

211

Patterns

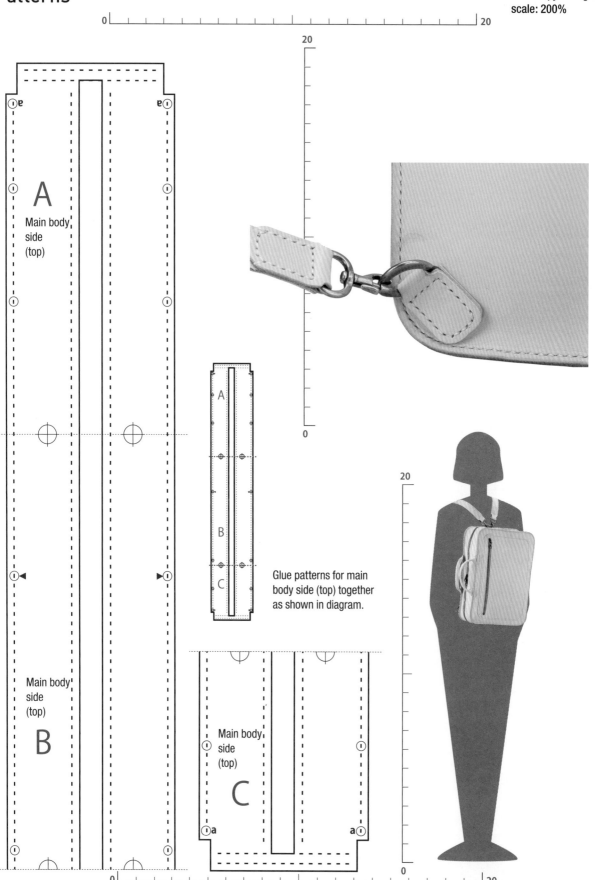

A Main body side (top)

B Main body side (top)

C Main body side (top)

Glue patterns for main body side (top) together as shown in diagram.

Patterns

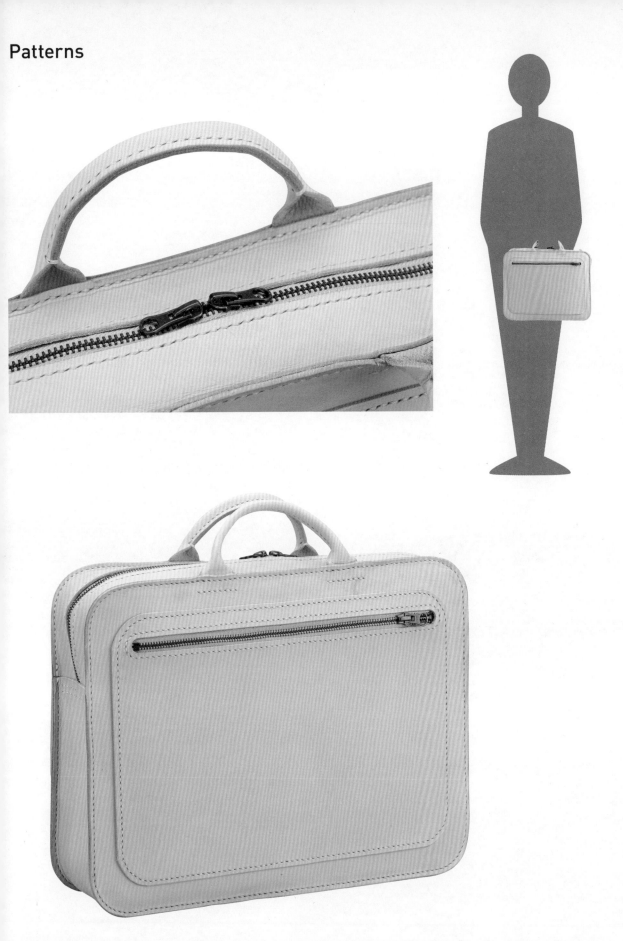

Leather Store and Workshop

This is what you'll find inside a specialty leather store. In this book, we make bags by using a single material called vegetable-tanned cowhide. However, there are many colored leathers that can be sewn by using the same patterns and techniques, thus creating bags with completely different expressions or even two-tone bags with the same design.

Leather is sold in sizes up to half a cowhide. You can spread out various large cowhides on a huge table and envision your bag in your mind while selecting the perfect piece of leather. You can also lay out patterns you brought with you to check their sizing, for example, at your convenience.

We have almost all the materials necessary for bag making, including **hardware, burnishing cream, leather cream, and hand-sewing thread.** We offer various types of leather such as pig, sheep, and goat—each with different textures and properties—as well as leather with lamé prints or embossing, which can stimulate your creativity.

The retro machine in the photo is a leather-cutting machine. With the correct mold, you can get sharply cut leather pieces—from really small parts, such as flowers or hearts, to small-sized bags.

Knowledgeable staff members who specialize in leather crafts are available to answer questions and provide advice, which is very helpful.

In workshops, you can choose from the many leathers available in the store and enjoy making bags of various designs.

©TAMURAKO
https://www.tamurakou.co.jp
2-19-11 Imado, Taito-ku, Tokyo 111-0024
TEL. 03-3874-4906 / FAX. 03-3874-4988
Email Address: tamura-co@jcom.home.ne.jp

Yoko Ganaha (PIGPONG)

PIGPONG is Yoko Ganaha and Piggy Tsujioka's arts-and-crafts production group. Product planning, book design, illustration, dyeing, creating objects, displays, etc.—pigpong delivers unique projects that are full of originality. https://www.sigma-pig.com/

English-edition copyright ©2025 by Schiffer Publishing, Ltd.

Library of Congress Control Number: 2024941287

Type set in DIN 2014/Helvetica Neue

ISBN: 978-0-7643-6876-9
Printed in China

Published by Schiffer Publishing, Ltd.
4880 Lower Valley Road
Atglen, PA 19310
Phone: (610) 593-1777; Fax: (610) 593-2002
Email: info@schifferbooks.com
Web: www.schifferbooks.com

For our complete selection of fine books on this and related subjects, please visit our website at www.schifferbooks.com. You may also write for a free catalog.

Schiffer Publishing's titles are available at special discounts for bulk purchases for sales promotions or premiums. Special editions, including personalized covers, corporate imprints, and excerpts, can be created in large quantities for special needs. For more information, contact the publisher.

First designed and published in Japan in 2021 by Graphic-sha Publishing Co., Ltd.
1-14-17 Kudan-Kita, Chiyoda-ku, Tokyo 102-0073, Japan
Japanese edition © 2021 Graphic-sha Publishing Co., Ltd.
All rights reserved.

Original-edition creative staff
SUPERVISOR: TAMURAKO
                                         KIYOKO WATANABE (Planning Sales Department)
PHOTOGRAPHER: TAKAYUKI YOSHIZAKI
DESIGN AND ILLUSTRATION: YOKO GANAHA
Production Co-operation: PIGGY TSUJIOKA, MITSUE KOBAYASHI (PIGPONG),
                                         TAKAKO SUZUKI, KYOKO ASAKA (TAMURAKO)
Cooperation: KUMIKO KUROKAWA, HISAKO ROKKAKU
EDITOR: NAOKO YAMAMOTO (Graphic-sha Publishing)

English-edition creative staff
English translation: Kevin Wilson
English-edition layout: Shinichi Ishioka
Foreign-edition production and management: Takako Motoki, Yuki Yamaguchi (Graphic-sha Publishing)

Printed in China.